Jesus: God, Ghost or Guru?

About the Authors and Respondent

JON A. BUELL Jon Buell is vice president of Probe Ministries and executive editor of the Christian Free University Curriculum. He is a graduate of the University of Miami in communication arts and of the Institute of Biblical Studies. He has also served on the faculty of the Institute. Mr. Buell has been in student ministry since 1961, speaking and interacting with students on college and university campuses throughout the USA and Canada. He is a frequent guest lecturer in the classrooms of major universities. Mr. Buell's interaction with students on the deity of Christ led to his own study of the subject that has culminated in this book.

O. QUENTIN HYDER Quentin Hyder maintains a private psychiatry practice in New York City and is Medical Director of the Christian Counseling and Psychotherapy Center in midtown Manhattan. He is also involved in clinical research at the Columbia-Presbyterian Medical Center. Dr. Hyder received his M.D. from Cambridge University and the London Hospital and obtained his psychiatric training at Columbia University. He is a member of the American Psychiatric Association, the Christian Medical Society, and the Christian Association for Psychological Studies.

F. F. BRUCE F. F. Bruce has been Rylands Professor of Biblical Criticism and Exegesis, University of Manchester, since 1959. He has M.A. degrees from Aberdeen, Cambridge, and Manchester. In 1957 he received an honorary D.D. from Aberdeen. He is a Fellow of the British Academy. Dr. Bruce is editor of the *Palestine Exploration Quarterly* and *The Evangelical Quarterly*. He served as general editor of the eighteen-volume *New International Commentary on the New Testament*, writing the volumes on Acts and Colossians. Other books he has written include *The Spreading Flame* and *The New Testament Documents: Are They Reliable?*

Jesus: God, Ghost or Guru?

Jon A. Buell
and
O. Quentin Hyder

With a response by
F. F. Bruce

ZONDERVAN PUBLISHING HOUSE
OF THE ZONDERVAN CORPORATION
GRAND RAPIDS, MICHIGAN 49506

PROBE MINISTRIES
INTERNATIONAL
RICHARDSON, TEXAS 75080

Copyright © 1978 by Probe Ministries International

Library of Congress Cataloging in Publication Data

Buell, Jon A
  Jesus: God, Ghost or Guru?

  (Christian free university curriculum)
  Bibliography: p.
  1. Jesus Christ—Person and offices—Addresses, essays, lectures. I. Hyder, O. Quentin, 1930- joint author. II. Bruce, Frederick Fyvie, 1910- joint author. III. Title. IV. Series.
  BT202.B79   232   78-15100

ISBN 0-310-35761-6

Place of Printing *Printed in the United States of America*

Permissions

page 33 Used with permission of Macmillan Publishing Company, Inc., from Macmillan Bible Atlas by Yohanon Aharoni and Michale Avi-Yonah, copyright © 1964, 1966, 1968, 1977 by Carta Limited

page 44 Courtesy of John Rylands University Library of Manchester

page 58 Courtesy of Three Lions, Inc., New York

page 106 Adapted from *Flatland: A Romance of Many Languages,* by Edwin A. Abbott. 5th ed., rev. New York: Barnes & Noble, p. 77

Scripture quotations are from the New American Standard Bible, © The Lockman Foundation 1960, 1962, 1963, 1968, 1971, 1972, 1973, 1975, and are used by permission.

Design Cover design by Paul Lewis
Book design by Louise Bauer

What Is Probe?

Probe Ministries is a nonprofit corporation organized to provide perspective on the integration of the academic disciplines and historic Christianity. The members and associates of the Probe team are actively engaged in research as well as lecturing and interacting in thousands of university classrooms throughout the United States and Canada on topics and issues vital to the university student.

Christian Free University books should be ordered from Zondervan Publishing House (in the United Kingdom from The Paternoster Press), but further information about Probe's materials and ministries may be obtained by writing to Probe Ministries International, Box 5012, Richardson, Texas 75080.

Contents

Illustrations

Book Abstract

A widespread debate over the past century has focused on the identity of Jesus. Was the assertion of his deity superimposed upon him by others or was it his own self-representation? Several lines of inquiry revealing that he personally claimed deity are explored. Based on this knowledge, an examination is made of three possible explanations for Jesus' assertion: 1) he was deliberately misrepresenting his identity, 2) he was sincere but deluded, and 3) he was sincere and correct.

chapter one

Close Encounter of Which Kind?

The question of Jesus' deity is raised and his own self-conception identified as primal evidence. The chapter discusses briefly the question about historical knowledge: Is it possible to reconstruct remote events so as to know the truth about them?

Recently I took part in a series of lectures in classes at Michigan State University. Included in my assignments was a request to speak in a philosophy of science class. This session with a small group of students soon proved to be one of the most lively of the series. Just six or seven minutes into the lecture, I was interrupted by a student who was obviously rather unhappy with my emerging viewpoint. We never made it back to the lecture, but our discussion was at least as productive as the lecture would have been.

The conversation immediately following his interruption was a dialogue that has been repeated, with 11 minor variations, innumerable times between the materialist and the theist (usually the biblical theist). More often than not, it goes something like this:

Materialist: Wait a minute. You used the word *God.* I take it you mean a personal, all-powerful kind of God.

Theist: Yes, that's what I meant.

Materialist: Well, I don't deny your right to believe in such a God, but unless you can prove His existence to me, it's obvious that He's only part of your religious or philosophical bias.

Theist: Why do you call it a bias?

Materialist: Because all the evidence we have tells us that reality is regular and predictable in its operation and that everything is explainable in terms of natural laws.

Theist: I'm not denying the operation of natural law, nor its "reign" over nature. That is a reality. I'm simply saying that there is something besides this material reality, or beyond it, if you wish, that is really real.

Materialist: And that's exactly what I'm referring to as your bias. After all, can you produce any *evidence* for your reality "beyond the material"?

Unfortunately, the conversation often ends there, or detours just short of its logical conclusion. In fact, the theist cannot produce any evidence of another reality "out there" beyond our present material realm; no one has ever invented a telescope (or "spiritscope!") that can penetrate beyond the natural realm. We have no way of detecting anything beyond the natural sphere.

But the logical conclusion of the dialogue, and the point often missed, is that this absence of information deprives the theist and the materialist equally. The "scope" that could provide empirical evidence for whatever is there, is just as necessary to establish that it is missing. And so, our friends are left stalemated in a stubborn dilemma—the theist can produce no evidence for; the materialist, none against. Based strictly on our present capacity to search out, detect, and gather the evidence, then, we really cannot know.

Now the materialist—the thoroughgoing atheist—takes this as his cue to affirm the materialistic view. Like the stubborn fisherman with the two-inch mesh net, he says, "What my net won't catch ain't fish." He disavows any possibility of some small variety of fish that his net is *incapable* of catching. This is as much a faith position as the one that the theist holds. However, for the person wishing to base his view on evidence (a legitimate wish, to say the least), agnosticism is a consistent view to hold—unless there is another possibility. And there is. Suppose for a moment that the supernaturalist is correct. Then there is one final option: that God, whatever He may be like, could recognize our inability to make contact with Him and take the initiative to communicate with us. A kind of cosmic "don't call us; we'll call you."

Please allow me to be repetitious. It is only when we see how inadequate is our knowledge of the "beyond," how absolute is our inability to improve on that knowledge, and therefore how honestly grounded we are philosophically, that we begin to sense the weight and magnitude of this final possibility. That is, that God, if He is there, would be able and willing to penetrate the material realm from the outside in. The philosophical term for such an action is *revelation,* a disclosure that is not dependent on our philosophical or technological capacities.

Now, if we are to entertain the possibility that God could penetrate "the veil" and establish contact with us—and certainly we must, to be philosophically fair—then the next question to consider is, "Has He ever done so?"

Of the several claims currently made concerning revelations, it is interesting that so many are private. This is the position of the mystic, who claims privileged knowledge from the beyond. Several of the contemporary cults are based on such knowledge from "visions," private appearances, etc. In a day when public sentiment runs strong for tolerance and plurality, it is important to recognize how fiercely exclusive are such claims to private knowledge. One person "has a vision" or "hears God's voice," and we are all asked to trust that person, with no way to check the validity of his claim. Understandably, most people today will require evidence supporting any such claim.

**The Question
Raised**

And that brings us to the purpose of this book. Much in our society and culture presents us with the claim that Jesus of Nazareth was, and is, God. An impressive amount is known about Jesus as a matter of historical fact. The locations of many of the major events and discourses of his life are visible today, although there is some ambiguity and competition concerning sites. Independent source materials about his life and teachings come to us from his contemporaries, both friend and foe. Also, Palestinian archaeology has expanded our knowledge of the culture of Jesus' day to vast proportions. Furthermore, books, articles, and art forms portraying, discussing, or describing the life of this individual have poured forth in an unending stream for nearly twenty centuries. Concerning the life of no other man of antiquity is such a glut of detail within the common knowledge. But one question remains: *Who was he?*

Oh yes, opinions on the subject are within easy reach. A fifteen-minute survey of people nearby will turn up a smorgasbord of ideas.

"A great man—ahead of his times."

"God the Son, the third Person of the Trinity."

"A benign maniac; you know, just a Jewish extremist—a troubled man."

"A kind of Western guru—in touch with the universe."

"A Beloved Invader, someone who can change your life."

"I don't know . . . a superstar, I guess."

And on it will go.

Songwriter Tim Rice put the question rhetorically to Jesus himself: "Jesus Christ, Superstar, do you think you're who they say you are?" Nor is the query only so much doctrinal chatter. Rather, it is a vital and foundational question. The purpose of this book is to provide the thoughtful reader with an opportunity to set aside the smorgasbord and to weigh carefully and critically the pertinent evidence, evidence that is available to each of us.

However, before we enter that process of evaluation, let's clear away some potentially dangerous debris from our path. It is hardly a secret that many people have strong feelings on the subject of religion in general and the deity or humanity of Christ in particular. Thus, it is possible to carry prior beliefs—strong personal preferences—*to* the evidence itself. (The reader may have already felt a fresh twinge from his own particular set of preferences, even though we have not yet begun our study.) It is a fairly common understanding that such prior beliefs have a commanding power to color one's perception of the evidence and consequently to hinder one's capacity to come to reliable conclusions.

Unfortunately, there is also a popular fallacy afoot today that equates religious commitment with subjectivity and champions the person who has broken all ties with orthodoxy as the only one who can be truly objective and free of all prior beliefs. G. R. Driver (who is not a spokesman for the orthodox view) has an insightful comment:

> Those who hold such views [. . . that agnosticism *per se* confers a lack of bias, an absolute impartiality unattainable by other men, and that "only an independent scholar, not committed to any religion" can be trusted to give an unbiased and independent opinion where questions of religion are involved . . .]* are apparently unaware that unbelief is as much a *praejudicium* as belief, that suspended judgment may be due to nothing else than sloth, and that the tabula rasa of a mind which they admire as a guarantee of disinterested scholarship can hardly exist in a normal man.[1]

Knowingly or otherwise, adherents of this fallacy have

---

*The parenthetical material is from an earlier paragraph and is quoted here by way of explanation.

made themselves at least as vulnerable, if not more so, to the distorting influence of personal preferences as those they criticize. Although he had a completely different topic in mind, David Bohm's counsel is relevant:

> It seems clear that everybody has got some kind of metaphysics, even if he thinks he hasn't got any. Indeed, the practical "hardheaded" individual who "only goes by what he sees" generally has a very dangerous kind of metaphysics, i.e., the kind of which he is unaware . . . dangerous because, in it, assumptions and inferences are being mistaken for directly observed facts, with the result that they are effectively riveted in an almost unchangeable way into the structure of thought.[2]

It would seem, then, that the best way to defuse the "bias bomb" is through exposure, beginning with our acknowledgment of whatever we perceive our prior beliefs to be and continuing with a healthy dose of other views. A final comment worthy of note comes from Oscar Cullmann, certainly no spokesman for orthodoxy.

> It is regrettable that also in this purely exegetical question [of Jesus' deity as presented in the New Testament] the decision usually depends upon the "theological standpoint" of the scholar; and here again it is not only the "conservative," but also just as much the opposite attitude which often influences exegesis.[3]

**You Can
Get There
From Here**

Another question that may break our concentration is simply the nagging query, can we ever really know the truth about Jesus of Nazareth? Is there any way to fight our way back through the tangled centuries of time and the myriads of beliefs, interpretations, traditions, and copy upon copy of historical material—most doubtless designed to communicate, and yet more often than not serving to obscure the original stage of history to the inquisitive eye? We may even despair of any real way of knowing. Over the past century some authors have despaired, concluding in their "quest for the historical Jesus" that there is no evidence to provide firm footing for a conclusion.

However, throughout the same period, archaeology and historical inquiry have enriched and increased our knowledge dramatically.

Not long ago, I had the helpless feeling of one who could only stand by while tragic circumstances unfolded for a friend. Three college students had filed a flight plan and then had taken a light aircraft on a northwesterly course across Arkansas. Their plane never landed at its anticipated destination, and in the uncertain hours that followed, no reports of radioed distress messages broke the agonizing silence for parents and friends. Day after day the reports were the same: "No information—no progress."

Days stretched into weeks, with still no clues, and the families of the young men had to return to work. However, every weekend my friend returned to rural Arkansas and searched for eyewitnesses, hoping that even weeks after the flight someone might recall seeing a plane with the color and markings of this one. Even one such recollection might provide a clue that would lead eventually to the location of the plane and students. Weekend after weekend of work, travel, and laborious questioning of potential observers finally began to bear fruit. One recollection after another helped to reconstruct the actual course of flight taken by the plane. Soon there began to emerge a sketchy picture of storm clouds necessitating a detour—a detour so costly in fuel consumption that it had to be forsaken. The pilot apparently had turned back, hoping that behind him he would find a landing strip within reach of his fuel capacity. Tragically, he never did. But the process of inquiry finally led to the discovery of the wrecked plane.

Besides the heart-rending loss, the remarkable feature of this story is the relentless search of my friend and the classic example it represents of how an event of the past can be recaptured. It was an impressive demonstration of the effectiveness of his method of reconstruction—discovering the truth about a past event. Eyewitness testimony was corroborated, modified, enriched, and confirmed as observer after observer added his firsthand account to the emerging picture. The truth could be known, though not without painstaking inquiry.

It is no less true with our topic: discovering the truth about the identity of Jesus. There may have been a time when those unwilling to rely on the "believing reports" of the Gospels were unduly hindered in their search by a scarcity of extrabiblical testimony. It is not so today. We can superimpose and compare the testimony of the eyewitnesses and their contemporaries, of firsthand observers and those who had access to the public knowledge they established, of the loyal, the hostile, and the utterly indifferent. When we do so, it is possible to get a coherent picture, overwhelmingly consistent with the vast majority of this primary-source data. As we proceed in our discussion, we will attempt to grant only what can be thus supported.

The Claim

Our entry into the question must begin with a careful look at what Jesus claimed about himself. All of humanity's great teachers sooner or later are asked about themselves, and it is no different with Jesus. Jesus' self-conception will never serve as tie-breaking evidence, but it is the proper place to begin. If this primal element can be established, other possible evidences can then be checked for consistency, as the historical picture develops and expands.

Did Jesus exhibit the belief that he was a word—a communication—from "beyond"? Clearly, this is what Jesus intended when he said: "Not that any man has seen the Father, except the One who is from God, He has seen the Father" (John 6:46). "I and the Father are one" (John 10:30). "You are from below, I am from above; you are of this world; I am not of this world" (John 8:23). By these and many other statements, as well as through his behavior, he claimed to be a revelation.

But, as spectacular as this assertion was, his claims went beyond this. He claimed that the special means of revelation in his case was that God was actually visiting planet Earth. Much more than simply an envoy with a divine message—which has certainly been a

common claim by men throughout history—Jesus left
no doubt with his hearers; he was seizing title to deity
itself. He said he was God incarnate (clad in human
flesh).

A little reflection will underscore for us how uncommon is any such claim. Admittedly, several have
claimed it. And some do today. Institutions are full of
such people. But among the serious teachers of
humanity—those whose lives and teachings evoked
sober consideration from their hearers—we search
long and hard for a parallel. Look, for example, at
Muhammad. No man ever waged more deliberate ef-
forts to generate a new religion. Yet if his zealous
followers ever went overboard and tried to worship
him, Muhammad recoiled. The Koran attributes no
miracles to him; what's more, in it Muhammad de-
clares to the "people who have knowledge" that he is
"only a mortal, like them."[4] No, Islam sees a claim to
deity by *any* person (including Muhammad) as
shirk—the single unpardonable sin.

As his death approached, Buddha was asked how he
wished to be remembered; in reply,

> he simply urged his followers not to trouble themselves
> about such a question. It did not matter much whether
> they remembered him or not, the essential thing was the
> teaching—and what mattered about the teaching was the
> *Way,* to live so that at last, in this life or later, illumination
> and release would be ours too. It is almost, in this regard,
> like a scientific doctrine; it does not matter at all that much
> who propounded it provided we can understand it and use
> it now.[5]

But is wasn't so with Jesus. Today tens of millions of
Christians take part in communion services—
picturing the internalizing of that revelation. Why? All
because Jesus instructed his followers to use this simple ceremony to aid in *remembering him* (Luke 22:19).
Jesus made the most spectacular claims of any serious
teacher of humanity. Without parade or fanfare, and
yet forthrightly, he claimed to be God. E. O. James
says:

> The Godhead attributed to the founder of Christianity,

alike in the New Testament and by the church, renders it unique in the history of religion. Nowhere else had it ever been claimed that a historical founder of any religion was the one and only supreme deity.[6]

However, before proceeding further, it is appropriate to clarify one point that any investigator will want adequately answered. It is not uncommon to hear someone in a bull session state that Jesus himself never claimed to be God. "He claimed to speak for God," the view goes, "and he was a great teacher, but he didn't say he was God. That was superimposed on him by devoted followers as sufficient time passed for the growth of such myths."

Why is it that such a view, now impossible in light of the present state of historical knowledge, is still offered in serious discussion? It is because of an unfortunate gap in communication between what we *can* know and what we in fact *do* know. The scholarship that has dismissed this mistaken notion is now a part of what we could call "public knowledge" and will be discussed in the rest of this book. However, public knowledge is something quite other than common knowledge, and regrettably, the economics of sensationalism play a major role in this communication gap.

A case in point (although not the first) is the high sales performance of Schonfield's *Passover Plot*. Thousands picked up a copy of this popular paperback and read in it Schonfield's contention that Jesus claimed to be the long-awaited Jewish Messiah, but not God. It should be obvious that many of Schonfield's readers had not, and have not since, read any of the formidable scholarly material (from both liberal and conservative scholars alike) that has made this popular fallacy untenable. Thus Schonfield's credentials, which seem adequate enough, combine with the high market performance of sensational books to keep modern man in the shadows.

chapter two

Jesus' Self-Conception

Jesus' words, his behavior, and the responses of his audiences are considered as areas of evidence concerning his claim. A major section is devoted to tracing the Old Testament development of the "theophanic formula" and the use Jesus made of this phrase of divine revelation.

The popularity of *The Passover Plot* is ample testimony to the fact that, long after a robust idea has died a natural death, its ghost lingers on. Indeed, some are finally banished only with great travail. This is certainly the case with the idea that Jesus did not claim deity—an idea that is still popularly accepted.*

---

*The reader who has no misgivings about the authenticity of Jesus' claims to deity may understandably feel that this chapter strains to document the obvious. It is not our intention to belabor the point, but the lingering popularity of the idea that Jesus did not claim deity calls for a careful autopsy.

Before we approach Jesus' explicit words, however, consider that, in many human situations, how a person *behaves* is more telling evidence of his intentions or contentions than what he *says*. For example, we often hear a mother exert her authority by threatening to spank her three-year-old if he doesn't quiet down. Sometimes several threats are given, but no spanking. It's her action of spanking the child that would really be convincing. In a similar way, we should expect to see in Jesus' life style indications that he *behaved* as if he were God. (Whether he did so in a calculated and deceitful manner is a question we will reserve for chapter four.)

One such act was Jesus' pronouncement of pardon, as seen, for example, in Mark 2. Early in Jesus' Galilean ministry, a paralytic was lowered by his friends through a hole in the roof to Jesus' feet. Jesus' initial response seemed quite beside the point (until he later healed the paralytic): "My son, your sins are forgiven." We must not miss the boldness of his words: he never consulted the injured parties, yet almost cavalierly declared that whatever the paralytic had done to others (while Jesus wasn't even around!) was now forgiven. C. S. Lewis, the great Cambridge scholar of English literature, rightly exclaims:

> Now it is quite natural for a man to forgive something you do to *him*. Thus if somebody cheats *me* out of £5 it is quite possible and reasonable for me to say, "Well, I forgive him, we will say no more about it." What on earth would you say if somebody had done you out of £5 and I said, "That is all right, I forgive him"?[7]

It may be argued, as by Lane,[8] that Jesus' pronouncement of pardon was not clearly a claim to deity, since he may have intended his words to be like those of a prophet who only announces a divine pardon for God (2 Sam. 12:13). However, the response of the scribes who are present is not to question Jesus' credentials as a prophet. Instead they object (Mark 2:7), "Why does this man speak that way? He is blaspheming; who can forgive sins but God alone?" From this response it seems clear that the most obvious interpre-

tation of Jesus' words in Mark 2:5 is that they imply
use of *his own* divine authority. Nevertheless, even if
we were to grant that Jesus' behavior here is not completely clear in its meaning, later in this chapter we will
appeal to his explicit words for clarification. It is
sufficient now to show that this behavior would be
consistent with any explicit claim to deity.

We have mentioned that the basic thesis of *The
Passover Plot* is that Jesus did not claim deity, but did
claim to be Israel's prophesied and long-awaited Messiah. Yet, there isn't a single verse in the Old Testament (or other Jewish literature) that clearly designates
for the Messiah the power to forgive sins, although the
same literature does ascribe this power to Jehovah! In
pardoning sin, then, Jesus was asserting the ascribed
power of deity, not that of messiahship. Overlooking
this is typical of the numerous inadequacies of
Schonfield's thesis.

Hand in hand with this feature of Jesus' behavior
was his portrayal of himself as the ultimate judge. It is
interesting that people will sometimes maintain they
don't believe in the Jesus of John's Gospel, with all his
claims to deity, but that they do feel that the Jesus who
gave us the Sermon on the Mount is authentic. At the
close of the Sermon on the Mount (Matt. 7:21-23),
Jesus presents himself as the one to whom many would
say in the day of judgment, "Lord, Lord, did we not
prophesy in Your name. . . ?" (Matt. 7:22). He
would then deny that he ever knew them, and they
would be judged accordingly.

Throughout his ministry, Jesus was consistent with
this theme. In fact, we find him at the close of his
ministry standing indicted before the supreme court of
Israel, still portraying his central role in the final judgment, as we shall see later in the chapter. Both
behaviors—forgiving and presenting himself as the
ultimate judge—imply an authority greater than that of
any mere human.

A second major line of evidence that comes to us **Audience
most often, in a delicate interplay with his divine **Response**

behavior, is the response Jesus drew from his hearers. We can be certain that when Jesus said, "I and the Father are one" (John 10:30), nobody drawled, "Now that's an interesting philosophical alternative." No, instead they picked up rocks, according to John, fully intending to make a rock pile out of him. This intention was in accord with the law, which called for capital punishment for anyone claiming deity[9] (based on their assumption that this statement was false).

This response, however, is but one of two opposite responses that consistently follow Jesus during his tour of ministry. The other, of course, is worship. Both responses are seen in all four Gospels. Take, for example, Matthew's account of Jesus in the temple in chapter 21. He had just been hailed with "Hosanna" from the multitude—as he approached Jerusalem on a donkey (the Triumphal Entry). After he drove the money-changers out of the temple, children in the temple picked up the theme and cried out, "Hosanna to the Son of David!"; i.e., "Help us, Son of David!" (Matt. 21:15).

Does Jesus take their cries as worship? Certainly wherever Jesus perceives someone is worshiping him, it is of special interest to us, because it constitutes an opportunity for Jesus to clarify his identity—to make a further statement about it. Does he hush the children? Does he recoil in horror at the sight of people worshiping a mere man? To be sure, the enculturated mind-set of the Jew would react reflexively against any misplaced worship. We see this clearly in Paul's response to the mistaken worship of the people of Lystra in Asia Minor, for example (Acts 14:8-15).

Matthew records in verses 15 and 16 that the chief priests and scribes, upon hearing the children, are indignant at the delay in Jesus' response. They urge him to reject the foolishness of the children. But Jesus' response is startling. Instead of recoiling, he asks if they have never read in Psalm 8:2, "Out of the mouth of infants and nursing babes *Thou* hast prepared praise for Thyself" (Matt. 21:16). Jesus is not only acknowledging their enthusiasm as praise, but he is justifying that praise on the basis of a psalm (in the Septuagint—

the common version of the day) that proclaims that God had prepared it for Himself.

Jesus never brandishes a scepter nor seeks fanfare. He even avoids crowds on several occasions because in their enthusiasm they want to make him their king. Nevertheless, in account after account, he receives the quiet statements and acts of devotion and worship of his contemporaries almost matter-of-factly. The acclaim of Peter (Matt. 16:16) and of the hold-out Thomas (John 20:28), the worship of the disciples afloat on the Sea of Galilee (Matt. 14:33) and again just prior to their being commissioned by Jesus to go and make disciples of all nations (Matt. 28:17), and the anointing with costly perfumed ointment by the woman in Bethany (Mark 14:3-9) are but a few of the many occasions when Jesus commended those who worshiped him.

It is nearly impossible to miss the harmony between Jesus' behavior as one who possesses divine authority and the answers of both rage and devotion with which his hearers responded. This picture of consistency is rich in historical detail and documentation.

Although the harmony that exists between Jesus' divine behavior and the response of his hearers is impressive, shouldn't we expect to see something more, if Jesus is claiming deity? Just how he might make it clear to us is not easy to predict, but in addition to the foregoing implications based on his behavior we would expect to find some overt assertions by Jesus. Somehow we would not want him to overdo it, but nevertheless shouldn't we hear from his own lips that this is indeed his conception of himself? Mark 12:35-37 is an important passage in this regard. In this incident, reported by each of the synoptic Gospels, we find Jesus discussing the meaning of Psalm 110:1 with the scribes and Pharisees (Mark 12:35-37):

Direct Claims

> And Jesus answering began to say, as He taught in the temple, "How *is it that* the scribes say that the Christ is the son of David? David himself said in the Holy Spirit,
> 'The Lord said to My Lord,

"Sit at My right hand, until I
put Thine enemies beneath Thy feet." '
"David himself calls Him 'Lord'; and *so* in what sense is
He his son?" And the great crowd enjoyed listening to
Him.

The question Jesus puts to them is designed to
stretch their concept of the Christ, or Messiah. A
familiar designation for Messiah was "son of David,"
yet if David, writing Psalm 110 a millennium earlier,
wrote, "The LORD [Yahweh or Jehovah] said unto *my*
Lord" (Adonai—taken commonly to be a reference to
the Messiah), then the scribes and Pharisees were
confronted with David (to their thinking, writing under
the inspiration of the Spirit) calling his own descendant
"Lord" (Adonai). Jesus' question is how the scribes
and Pharisees can reconcile this apparent discrepancy.

He is not denying that the Messiah is a descendant of
David, nor is he questioning the scribal tradition of
designating the Messiah as "son of David"; this tradition was firmly rooted in Old Testament teaching. But,
since David was held as the highest of the kings of the
earth (Ps. 89:27), Jesus was showing them how out of
keeping it was for David to refer to any other human as
"Lord." Thus he probes their concept of a purely
human Messiah as opposed to a divine one. It is typical
of Jesus, in claiming to be the Messiah, to extend the
messianic concept to include divine attributes, as he
has done here.

**Jehovah's
Phrase of
Self-revelation**

We come next to what perhaps represents the most
conclusive evidence concerning Jesus' assertion. Indeed, it may well be the most decisive way possible for
him to have made a claim to deity. It could be argued
that Jesus' concept of the Messiah was merely an
aberration of his own theology. Nevertheless, Jesus
dispels any remaining uncertainty by his deliberate and
persistent use of the short Hebrew phrase *Ani hu*,
meaning "I am He."

No one has more fully or lucidly laid out the evidence on this point than has Ethelbert Stauffer (cer-

tainly no spokesman for conservative theology) in the

final chapter of *Jesus and His Story*. Stauffer shows,
step by step, the rich history of meaning in this phrase
of revelation, and then demonstrates that we find it on
Jesus' lips again and again. Termed by Stauffer the
"self-revelational theophanic formula," *Ani hu* is frequently used by Jehovah in the Old Testament to identify Himself to men. The Greek translation of these two
Hebrew words is *egō eimi*. However, a simple "it is I"
is also expressed by the same Greek words, carrying no
reference to deity at all. Jesus uses the words in this
sense, for example, in Matthew 14:27. Thus we must
look at the context when Jesus uses the phrase, to see if
the theophanic phrase of revelation is actually behind
what he says. ("Theophanic" refers to a manifestation
or appearance of God to man.)

Both words of the phrase have roots of similar use.
Ani or "I" is used by Jehovah in important passages of
self-disclosure such as Deuteronomy 5:16 and Psalm
50:7. *Hu* is the emphatic form of the personal pronoun
huah, meaning "He," often used as a substitute for
Yahweh. We see the two combined quite often, trans-
latable (depending on the context) as either "I am He"
or simply "I am."

Quoted here from the Qumran Isaiah scroll (selected
verses), Isaiah 43 is a prime example of the importance
of this succinct phrase.

Fear not, for I have redeemed you.
I have called you by your name, you are mine.
When you pass through the waters I will be with you
For I am the Lord, your God. . . .
Fear not, for I am with you. . . .
You are my witnesses, whom I have chosen.
That you may know and believe me, and understand that I
     am he.
Before me was no God formed,
Neither shall there be any after me.
I, I am the Lord,
And besides me there is no savior.
I have declared it [to Abraham]. . . .
And you are my witnesses.
I am God.
Yea, since the day was I am he. . . .

I am the Lord your Holy One
who made a way in the sea,
a path in the mighty waters. . . .
I, I am he
who blots out your transgressions for my own sake:
and I will not remember your sins.

Here we can see that *Ani hu* alternates as the refrain with "I am the Lord, your God," "I am the Lord," and "I am God."

This phrase of revelation had a prominent place in the celebration of the Jewish pilgrim feasts. These feasts were occasions when the expectations of the Jews reached their highest point. The Jews believed that one day Jehovah would manifest Himself and His salvation to them openly.[10] The feasts were particularly regarded as likely occasions for this manifestation. This sense of expectancy was created, to some significant measure, by the frequent use of *Ani hu* in the feast liturgies taken from portions of the Psalms, Isaiah, Deuteronomy, and other books of the Talmud.

For example, during the Sabbath of the Feast of Tabernacles, the Levites sang the Song of Moses, or Deuteronomy 32. This passage exhibits a typical use of "I am He," seen in verse 39, where it is coupled with Jehovah's declaration of uniqueness—that there is no God besides Him.

On each day of the feast the priests moved around the altar in the great temple (the place of God's unique presence) singing, *"Ani we hu"* and "Hosanna." Stauffer points out that the *we* was probably inserted to slightly change the *Ani hu,* which may have been too holy to utter without this slight change. A similar dilemma involved the use of the name *Yahweh,* or *Jehovah,* which, because of its extreme holiness, never crossed the lips of the devout Jew.[11] He suggests there may have been two groups in the procession chanting antiphonally, i.e., with responses. One group would give this slightly veiled announcement of God's presence, "I am He," and the other would respond with "Hosanna" ("Then help us!").

Another feast in which the phrase is prominent is the Passover, during which the Great Hallel (Psalms 113 to 118) was sung antiphonally by priests and people. In

each Jewish home, the liturgy of the feast continued
under the direction of the father. After recounting the
miracles of Jehovah on the night Israel was delivered
from Egypt, the father quoted Deuteronomy 26:8,
"And the LORD brought us out of Egypt . . . with signs
and wonders." Then he gave the following interpretation:

> The LORD brought us out of Egypt—not by an angel,
> not by a seraph, nor even by an envoy, but the Holy
> One, praised be He in his glory, he himself, as it is
> written:
> I will pass over the land. I will . . .
> I will, I, the Lord.[12]

At the last he underscored its meaning with finality and
beauty through the benediction "I and not an angel; I
and not a seraph; I and not the envoy; I the Lord, *I am
He* and no other."[13]

Before turning to Jesus' use of the phrase, it is
important to take note that it is deeply and uniquely
Hebrew. It gathers the full force of its meaning from
passage after passage of the Old Testament. Through
the influence of F. C. Baur and others, it has been
widely held for more than a century that Jesus' claims
to deity were superimposed upon him by followers
removed from Jesus himself and eager to "Hellenize"
(cast into the cultural terms of the Greco-Roman
world) a message that was otherwise too Jewish to
appeal to such a world. If this were so, they would
never have used such a deeply Hebrew phrase for that
very fabrication. One is hard put to picture the average
Roman citizen meditating on Deuteronomy 32 or
Psalm 43! No, the non-Jew of the first century would
not have grasped the meaning behind the use of *Ani hu,*
nor would anyone desiring to "Hellenize" Jesus have
remotely thought of using such a term.

On the other hand, the Jew of Jesus' day was quite
aware of the phrase. It was neither equivocal nor
obscure to him. Recall that the Hebrew culture had no
counterpart to our modern flood of literature. Whereas
we race through books and papers at high speeds, their

libraries centered around the Torah (or Law), the Prophets, and other Old Testament writings. The entire texts of these were digested and meditated upon repeatedly. Furthermore, Stauffer points out that in A.D. 20 Isaiah 40–45 was a prominently discussed passage, and *hu* was a favorite term for Jehovah. This, says Stauffer, is important background to the sayings of Jesus. We can be confident that the phrase used in Jesus' day would be clear, so clear, in fact, that people would react just as the Gospels record they did toward Jesus when he used the phrase.

"I Am He"

Each of Jesus' uses of the theophanic formula *Ani hu* recorded in the Gospels is linked with one of the two festival seasons, Passover or Tabernacles.[14] At feast time, Jesus seemed to dwell on the term incessantly. We will look at three examples.

First, the passage in Mark 13:6 should be considered. Here Jesus keeps the exclusiveness of the phrase intact, but applies it to himself. He warns his disciples that many charlatans will come, "saying, 'I am He!' and will mislead many" (Mark 13:6). The thing to notice is that Jesus says these counterfeits saying *"Ani hu"* will be impersonating *him*.

Next, let us consider his words in John 13, spoken to his disciples at the occasion of the Last Supper, which took place in the middle of Passover Week. Undoubtedly some will object to any reliance on John for historical detail, because of their belief that John was written very late—when memories were faded and when imaginations had elaborated to fill in the blank spaces. Others will point to the concept of Hellenization mentioned above, for which John's Gospel has been indicted by some theologians.

Nevertheless, for three reasons, the passage is offered here for analysis. First, it can no longer be seriously maintained that the element of our attention—the revelational phrase—is Hellenistic or, for that matter, anything but Jewish. Second, what we detect in John is in complete harmony with similar uses of the phrase in the other three Gospels. And third, in a

later section we deal at some length with the question
of the dates and reliability of the Gospels, including
John.

At the Last Supper, Jesus has just predicted his
betrayal by Judas by quoting Psalm 41:9; and then he
explains the reason for his prophecy: ''From now on I
am telling you before it comes to pass, so that when it
does occur, you may believe that I am He'' (John
13:19). Once again, Jesus makes deliberate use of
these words of revelation—the disclosure of deity.
Stauffer points out that the resemblance to Isaiah 42:9
is unmistakable, ''Behold, the former things have
come to pass, now I declare new things; before they
spring forth I proclaim them to you.''

In this chapter of Isaiah, as well as in Jesus' conversation, the intention in using prediction is that the
fulfillment of the prediction might serve as further
evidence of deity. It may be noted that the phrase is
spoken in the privacy of Jesus' close friends. This may
be because use of the phrase there, after they had
supper, was analogous to the liturgy of the Passover
conducted in the home, spoken of earlier. The Last
Supper was a celebration of the Passover meal. We
may wish for a more public declaration, however,
recognizing that such private assertions among friends
would be difficult, if not impossible, to verify.

We should recognize, however, the strong cir-
cumstantial evidence expressed later in the lives of
these disciples. Their proclamation of the same message, in the face of treacherous persecutions designed
to force them to recant, in itself constitutes confirming
evidence of the highest value.

This brings us to the final use of the potent *Ani hu*.
No context available in Palestine could constitute a
more public, more vulnerable arena for Jesus to dis-
cuss his identity than the official proceedings of the
supreme court of Israel, the Great Sanhedrin.

**Jesus' Claim
Goes on Record**

Throughout the years of Jesus' open ministry, he
was on a collision course with official Judaism, pro-
gressing steadily toward a crisis confrontation. A host

of attempts have been made to give explanations—other than the biblical one—for the increasing hostility of the priests and Pharisees toward Jesus. However, these attempts all fail at the important task of explaining the hour of crisis, the trial itself, without rewriting the script. This we have little freedom to do, if evidence is given its due weight.

As an example, an Israeli Supreme Court justice recently suggested that the ancient body of religious rule—a seventy-man court—was really trying to save Jesus from Rome.[15] This theory, like so many others, shows disregard for the confines of historical data. To accommodate such an idea, both biblical and extrabiblical evidence must be ignored—the brute existence of Jesus, the Sanhedrin, and Rome appearing to be the only admissible data.

But we have digressed. The hour of the trial has arrived. It is night, and the Sanhedrin has gathered at the palace of Caiaphas (see Figure 1), the high priest. Caiaphas is leading the Sanhedrin in seeking evidence through which they can do away with Jesus. The Jews have not possessed the power of capital punishment since the reorganization of Judea as a Roman province under the control of a procurator in A.D. 6.[16] The one exception is their retention of jurisdiction over the sanctity of the temple. Violations of that sanctity are subject to capital punishment by an act of the Sanhedrin. Nevertheless, they are justified in assuming that their recommendation of the death penalty on other grounds would be accommodated by Pontius Pilate.

The questioning of the ecclesiastical tribunal is insistent. Witnesses contend that Jesus made a statement three years earlier that he would destroy the temple (an obvious sacrilege) and rebuild, in three days, a temple not made with human hands. (A conviction on this charge, of course, would be the cleanest way to achieve their purposes. The testimony of the witnesses, however, is confused and contradictory. The poignant portrayal of this scene in the television film *Jesus of Nazareth* by Anthony Burgess [and the book based on it by William Barclay] brought out dramatically the restraining effect of Joseph of Arimathea and

Figure 1. Jerusalem, showing paths followed from Jesus' arrest (mid-right: Garden of Gethsemane) to his crucifixion (upper left: Hill of Golgotha). Probable sight of trial in Caiaphas's palace is at lower left. Other ministry sights include (upper left) the rediscovered Sheep's Pool.

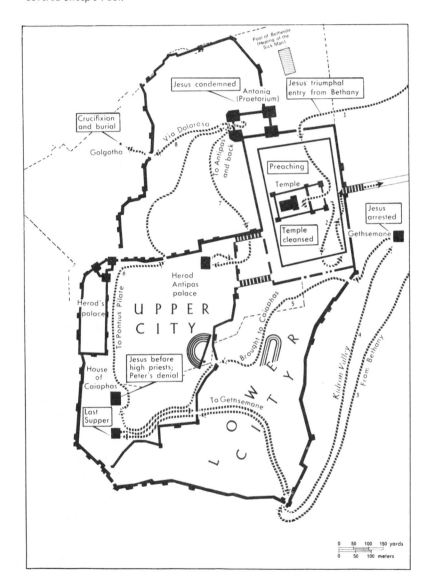

Nicodemus on the conduct of the prosecution.) The presence of these two men insures that the legal requirements of Jewish law be satisfied in full, so the contradictory testimony is thrown out.[17]

However, the pedantic, even slavish observance of the requirements of the law by Caiaphas does not deter his offensive. Finally, he rises to his feet and approaches Jesus, who has remained silent throughout the trial. As he does, the entire court also stands, as required by the protocol of the Sanhedrin. Although the allegations of Jesus' accusers (that he said he would destroy the temple and build a new one) cannot be used, they have a messianic "ring" to them, which provokes Caiaphas' final question. It is the one question Jesus cannot leave unanswered, "Are You the Christ, the Son of the Blessed *One?*" (Mark 14:61). (Caiaphas's phrase, "the Son of the Blessed One," was a popular Hebraism for the Messiah. "Blessed One" was a contraction of the phrase, "Holy One, blessed be He," referring to Jehovah; and the "Son" of this Blessed One was the Messiah.) So Caiaphas is not asking Jesus if he claims deity. He is asking, rather, if Jesus claims to be the Messiah.

A Stunning Reply

But Jesus gives Caiaphas all he can wish for and more. In Jesus' answer, he brings together the two concepts of messiahship and deity, and, under oath, lays full claim to both. "And Jesus said, 'I am [*Ani hu*]; and you shall see the Son of Man sitting at the right hand of Power, and coming with the clouds of heaven'" (verse 62). Jesus' words, though quiet, are stunning in their audacity. *Ani hu* in this passage is rendered simply "I am" in many translations, as if it were a simple reply to the "Are you . . . ?" of Caiaphas. However, it is the same phrase, used in the same way, that we have seen elsewhere translated "I am He." Surely Jesus realizes that his audience, intense in their quest for evidence against him, will interpret his words in the full sense of their theophanic meaning. It is a deliberate claim to deity, and, if not quite what Caiaphas has expected, an even greater blasphemy to his ears.

But Jesus makes it stronger still. Throughout his public ministry, he had used the phrase "Son of man." This was easily Jesus' favorite term of self-designation, and we find it quite frequently on his lips. The term is used in the book of Ezekiel, where it is a Hebraism for mere mortality. In his prophecy, Ezekiel exhibits a unique style, part of which is to recall the hearer to attention with questions such as: "Son of man, do you see what they are doing?" (Ezek. 8:6)

However, the prophecy of Daniel picks up the term and employs it for a much richer purpose. Specifically, Daniel 7 presents the Son of man as the one to whom is given an everlasting dominion over all people. This apocalyptic passage was taken as a prophecy of the future reign of Messiah.[18] Now, drawing on the imagery of Daniel 7, Jesus tells them that this imagery will one day actually occur in their view and that he will be the one to whom this everlasting dominion is given. The irony of Jesus' words should not be missed: although he is before them as one indicted and at their mercy, they, one day, will be at *his* tribunal, and he will be the judge. Bear in mind Jesus' reference (Mark 12:35-37) to Psalm 110:1, as discussed earlier, where he spoke with the Pharisees and scribes early in the week of his final Passover. At that time Jesus pointed out to the Pharisees that this passage, held by them and him to be messianic, teaches that David (who was to have no human superior) called the Messiah "Lord." It is with this understanding that he now places himself in the center of the scenario of Psalm 110:1, claiming that they, the members of the Great Sanhedrin, will see him "at the right hand of power."

Caiaphas's response is predictable outrage. "And tearing his clothes, the high priest said, 'What further need do we have of witnesses?' " (Mark 14:63). So there we have it. Jesus is given his chance to defend himself. The only question he answers is the question of his identity, and his answer is so unmistakable and incendiary that it is followed by the loud sound of tearing cloth. First, the high priest tears his robe with holy indignation at the blasphemy, then the court fills with the sound of tearing garments. Such a response to blasphemy is prescribed by the Mishnah.[19] Note that the great court is agreed that Jesus' reply is "deserving of death" (verse 64).

This judgment did not come because Jesus had claimed messiahship. The respected Jewish scholar Schoeps argues effectively that such a claim *could* not, and on other occasions by other men *did* not, bring such a judgment.[20] No, rather, the judgment came because he claimed deity. Regulations for conduct in the law set forth in the Pentateuch include the stipulation that blasphemy against God is worthy of death (Lev. 24:16). In addition, whoever arrogates to himself divine honors or privileges is held to be a blasphemer.[21]

Stauffer's concluding comments bear repeating:

> Judging by the linguistic form, the earlier history, and the content of the *"Ani hu"* formula, there can no longer be any doubt of what Jesus meant when he used it. He was in all deliberation using the Old Testament and liturgical formula of God's self-revelation. . . . The great event in the history of revelation had already taken place; God was present. . . . It was the boldest declaration. "I am He"—this meant: where I am there God is; there God lives and speaks, calls, asks, acts, decides, loves, chooses, forgives, rejects, suffers, and dies. Nothing bolder can be said, or imagined.[22]

In the Opinion of the Witnesses

We have looked at three lines of evidence that argue for the position that Jesus claimed deity: Jesus' behavior, the response of his audience, and his own overt claims. Before we look at the reliability of our information, which thus far has been drawn from the biblical documents, we will consider one final line of evidence that further strengthens the position under discussion: the considered conclusions of eyewitnesses.

Although we have already seen the response of various audiences of Jesus' ministry, it is worth distinguishing between these intermittent observers of his teachings and those whose eyewitness observations of Jesus' life and ministry were so extended and so keen that they ultimately led to the development of carefully

written reports. (The various questions raised concerning the authenticity, accuracy, and reliability of these reports will be discussed in the next chapter. Subsequent chapters will explore the various possibilities concerning the truth or error of Jesus' claim.)

Our interest at this point is in *what* the reports have to tell us. The evidence here is not always apparent at first. It is something like suddenly noticing an unfamiliar object in a room where you have spent a great deal of time, only to learn that the object has been there all along. The convictions of eyewitness observers, including Jesus' close associates, that he was God constitute good evidence in their own right that he did indeed make a claim to deity. Perhaps such convictions have previously been ruled inadmissible as evidence concerning the truth about Jesus on the basis that the Gospels are ''mere believing reports.'' Such an easy dismissal, however, cannot be justified. We may entertain the possibility that the writers were duped or mistaken, but we cannot rule out the alternative; we must give due weight to the ''belief'' of ''believing reports.''

We will limit ourselves to a very brief summary. It is of little additional use to go back and detail the evidence that Matthew, for example, held this view. We have spent a great deal of time documenting Jesus' claim from these primary documents. Matthew, Jesus' disciple, provided more than just eyewitness accounts at the request of the curious. After considering this matter carefully for many years, he had such a strong conviction about it that he took the time and effort to compose a Gospel account and, probably, even the *Logia* (sayings of Jesus recorded in Aramaic), as well. (Papias made a statement to this effect in A.D. 130—a statement that was later quoted by the historian Eusebius.)[23] The very fact that Matthew is our source is ample evidence that he believed in what he conveyed.

Of course, the same could be said for the other Gospels as well. However, some additional specifics are in order at this point. We have said little about the

Gospel of John, precisely to show that John is not at all necessary to establish that Jesus claimed to be God. Nevertheless, it is well to observe at this point that John refers to Jesus as the Word—"And the Word became flesh, and dwelt among us, and we beheld his glory . . . (John 1:14)—and sets the tone for the entire Gospel by a deliberate parallel to Genesis 1:1. In striking similarity, John 1:1 begins, "In the beginning was the Word, and the Word was with God, *and the Word was God.*"

Montgomery points out a telling feature of the opening passage of Mark's Gospel. (Mark was secretary to and close companion of Peter, and his Gospel could just as easily be called the Gospel of Peter.)

> At the very outset of this book Mark makes clear beyond all shadow of doubt that Jesus should be personally identified with the God of the Old Testament. He writes:
>> The beginning of the gospel of Jesus Christ, the Son of God. As it is written in the prophets, "Behold, I send my messenger before thy face, who shall prepare thy way; the voice of one crying in the wilderness: Prepare the way of the Lord, make his paths straight" (RSV, with marginal reading).
>
> Here Mark has quoted Malachi 3:1, but with a highly significant alteration. The prophetic verse reads:
>> "Behold, I [Jehovah] will send my messenger, and he shall prepare *the way before me.*"
>
> But Mark changes the verse so that it reads "he shall prepare *thy way,*" i.e., Jesus' way. Mark is saying, in other words, that when the God of the prophets spoke of preparing for His *own* coming, He was speaking of the preparation for Jesus' coming; or, putting it as simply as possible, Jesus *is* the God of the prophets.[24]

A Voice From the "Silent Years"

Finally, we come to the most remarkable eyewitness testimony of all: the book of James, written in all probability by James the brother of Jesus. Tradition attributes the book to him, and many lines of evidence adequately confirm the accuracy of this report. Yet, instead of parading his kinship to Jesus, James opens his book with the astonishing words, "James, a bondservant of God and of the Lord Jesus Christ. . ."

(James 1:1). If these lines are, in fact, penned by Jesus' brother, then we have a highly significant voice from the "silent years" of Jesus' life.

Here is one who played with Jesus when they were boys, romping over the hills near their simple Nazareth home; one who no doubt looked searchingly into his eyes as they faced, together with Mary and their brothers and sisters, the death of their father Joseph; one who shared countless times of grief and joy, not to mention the years of ordinary work, play, and growth experienced by any family. Which of us would expect to be so revered by his own brother or sister?

To summarize, we have seen a picture of formidable consistency as we have looked at four lines of evidence presenting the position that *Jesus claimed to be Messiah-God, the logos, or message to mankind from beyond the natural realm.* First, Jesus behaved as if he were divine (he forgave sins and claimed he would be involved in the final judgment of mankind). Second, his audience received his words as if he were claiming divinity. (Some worshiped him, while others accused him of blasphemy or urged him to reject the worship he was receiving.) Third, he quoted Scripture and religious terms regarding deity and applied them to himself. And, lastly, his close, long-term associates (including his own brother) became convinced that Jesus was God, some to the point of putting their convictions into writing.

We see a remarkable consistency in our sources concerning Jesus' claim to be God. Needless to say, the reliability of the sources that portray this picture is vital. In the chapter that follows we will take up the question, Can we really rely on the accuracy of our sources?

chapter three

A Tracer on
the Truth

Three major questions concerning the historical reliability and accuracy of the New Testament documents are posed. A summation of contemporary scholarship is given in each area.

Thus far, we have concentrated our attention on the *content* of Jesus' self-conception as reported to us primarily in the New Testament documents. The question has to be raised, of course, about the *reliability* of the reports that we are taking as our primary sources of information. If we could establish, first, that these sources are the substantially original form; second, that the reports were written by those who witnessed or were near to the events they recorded; and, third, that we could reasonably rely on the integrity of the witnesses, we would be justified in depending on the data thus received. 41

42

Jesus: God,
Ghost
or Guru?

Do We Have What
Eyewitnesses
Originally Wrote?

Many of us have visions of scribal monks gazing sleepily from beneath their hoods as they copied books of the Bible for countless hours in the early Christian era. In our mind's eye, we may see dim lighting, long hours, and slavish adherence to superstition combining to produce countless irretrievable errors in the process of transmitting the original down to our present version. We may ask if it is even possible to recapture the original reports at all.

It cannot be denied that we are dependent on a system of hand-copying for the transmission of the texts, a system that was still in use fifteen centuries following the life of Christ. It is also true that the advent of the printing press in the Renaissance made accuracy in reproducing copies of a text much easier. But it did not make accuracy more important. The high view of the New Testament documents held by the original Christian community meant the early development of a tradition of professional scribes, much as had been the case with their Jewish antecedents.

It is inevitable that in the volume of copies made of the New Testament documents, textual errors would creep in. However, that which is the source of the *problem*—the operation of chance through the sheer numbers of copies—is also the source of *solution*. A simple analogy will suffice to make this clear. Suppose that an English literature professor wrote on the blackboard a sonnet of his own composition, and then assigned his students the task of copying it, without error. There can be little doubt that some students— maybe even all—would make at least one or two minor errors. If the original on the blackboard were erased, would we then become hopelessly deadlocked by these errors in our attempt to reconstruct the original sonnet? Obviously, by comparing or superimposing many or all of the students' copies, we could readily eliminate the errors and could, with confidence, reproduce the sonnet exactly as the professor had written it on the board.

This pictures the essential position we are in when it comes to *textual criticism,* the study of the manuscript evidence itself. This evidence for the books of the New

Testament is remarkably good. All in all, there are some 5,340 Greek manuscripts in whole or in part to work with, covering a range of 1,400 years. Nor are we dependent only on recent copies. This number includes many that are undoubtedly first- and second-generation copies of the original texts. Two of the most important manuscripts are the Codex Vaticanus, at the Vatican Library, dating to the fourth century (ca. A.D. 350) and the Codex Sinaiticus, now displayed in the British Museum, also dating to the fourth century (ca. A.D. 350). These two codices (a codex is an ancient volume of manuscripts gathered into a book, as opposed to a scroll) each contain the entire Greek New Testament.

Another highly significant find was the discovery of the Chester Beatty Papyri shortly after the turn of the century. This collection of eleven papyrus codices includes three codices that, taken together, contain most of the New Testament writings. The codex containing the Gospels and the book of Acts dates to the first half of the third century (A.D. 200-250). A second, containing Paul's letters as well as the epistle to the Hebrews, dates as early.

Among the important New Testament fragments is the John Rylands Papyrus discovered in the early 1930s. It contains chapter 18, verses 31-33 and 37-40, of the Gospel of John. This is presently the oldest known surviving New Testament text, dating to A.D. 120-130. (See Figure 2, page 44.) Since it was found in Egypt, where it probably was copied, the original text had to have circulated for some reasonable period of time prior to that.

In addition to the thousands of whole or fragmented texts of New Testament books, we also have three other kinds of textual evidence to aid the task of reconstructing the originals. First, there are the quotations of New Testament passages—many at great length—by the early church leaders, or apostolic fathers, whose writings range from as early as A.D. 90 to 160 and thereafter. Examples of these are Clement, first-century bishop of Rome; Ignatius, bishop of Antioch; and Polycarp, who was taught by John the Apostle.

Together, these three patristic writers quote portions of the synoptic Gospels, the Gospel of John, Acts, Romans, 1 and 2 Corinthians, Galatians, Ephesians, Philippians, 2 Thessalonians, 1 and 2 Timothy, Titus, Hebrews, 1 Peter, and 1 John. Quotations from other New Testament books may also appear in their writings. A committee of the Oxford Society of Historical Theology collected the evidences of the apostolic fathers in 1905, publishing it in *The New Testament in the Apostolic Fathers.*[25] Much of the New Testament can be constructed from the writings of these apostolic fathers.

Figure 2. The John Rylands Papyrus, with parts of John 18, dating to A.D. *120-130.*

Second, over two thousand lectionaries have been recovered. These lectionaries are topical arrangements of Greek New Testament passages for reading in the church, written mainly in the seventh and eighth centuries.

Third, there is a variety of ancient translations of the New Testament. These include versions in Old Syriac and Old Latin dating back to the second half of the second century. Numbering over one thousand copies and fragments, these translations are found also in Coptic, Armenian, Gothic, and Ethiopic.

Together, the Greek manuscripts, the quotations of the apostolic fathers, the lectionaries, and the translations in other languages provide an extremely weighty and early witness to the original texts themselves. Frederic Kenyon, former Director and Principal Librarian of the British Museum, has summed up the question this way:

> The interval, then, between the dates of original composition and the earliest extant evidence becomes so small as to be in fact, negligible, and the last foundation for any doubt that the Scriptures have come down to us substantially as they were written has now been removed. Both the authenticity and the general integrity of the books of the New Testament may be regarded as finally established.[26]

B. F. Westcott and F. J. A. Hort, who provided a scholarly edition of the Greek New Testament before the beginning of the twentieth century, could say, on the weight of far less manuscript evidence than we now possess:

> If comparative trivialities such as changes of order, the insertion or omission of the article with proper names, and the like are set aside, the words in our opinion still subject to doubt can hardly amount to more than a thousandth part of the New Testament.[27]

We might add that none of that minute portion of the New Testament still subject to doubt bears on the claims that Jesus made for himself. We can be confident that what we read about Jesus' self-

**Were the
Original Reports
Written by
Eyewitnesses or
Those Near to the
Recorded Events?**

conception in our New Testament today is what was recorded in the original autographs or writings.

An honest approach, then, to the manuscript evidence through textual comparison, has brought about a general acceptance, even among the most skeptical theologians. Even historians who were religiously disinterested have admired the abundance and quality of the evidence. The discussion concerning the credentials of the original authors and their credibility, however, has been more spirited. We will give greater attention to detail, therefore, as we look at the evidence for eyewitness composition of the records, particularly where the records touch on some aspect of Jesus' self-disclosure.

The proposition that underlies this whole debate is, of course, that the longer the distance in time between any event and the recording of that event, the greater will elaboration, embellishment, and imagination play a part in the telling of that event. This is especially true if events are recorded, not by eyewitnesses, but on the basis of subsequent hearsay.

As the famous liberal British theologian John A. T. Robinson introduces his discussion of the subject, he remarks, "The *span* of time over which the New Testament is thought to have been written has expanded and contracted with fashion."[28] Such fashion began with the teachings of F. C. Baur, professor of theology at the University of Tübingen.

During the middle of the nineteenth century, Baur adapted the basic dialectic of Hegel to his own view that the original Christianity of Jesus and his disciples, especially Peter and James, was a fiercely Jewish thesis, and that it came into conflict with the somewhat later and broader Christianity of Paul, which was the antithesis. Out of this conflict, said Baur, came the synthesis, and thus early Catholicism was born with the accompanying New Testament books.

Baur derived dates for the New Testament manuscripts, not on the basis of objective criteria or scientific dating techniques, but *on the amount of time his theory required* to produce the specific vintage of theology contained in a given New Testament book. For example, John's Gospel, representing the synthesis, was dated by Baur as late as A.D. 170.

This teaching, known as the Tübingen school, dominated the thinking of liberal theologians for decades. However, the work of Cambridge professor J. B. Lightfoot, later that century, completely dispelled the powerful but arbitrary construct of Baur, and no theologian gives it credence today. The underlying ideas, nevertheless, have never been set aside, as various attempts have been made to demonstrate a divided origin for Christianity, if not one of open conflict.

Most liberal theologians today recognize that there was not time for the Hegelian dialectic to operate prior to the composition of the New Testament documents. However, the concept that has captured the allegiance of many of these theologians is the idea that Paul's message was aimed at the Gentile, the Hellenized citizen of the Roman world. As a consequence, many hold, Paul's teaching took a "Jewish" story and Hellenized it through the *kerygma*—the proclamation of the gospel—modifying it to appeal to the Gentile. Thus entered the claim to deity that, though a bane to Jewish ears, was patently Hellenistic—yes, even necessary to commend Jesus in a world that was accustomed to the idea of worshiping men as gods.

But this scheme too is dependent on some lapse of time between the life of Jesus and the development of such a message. How the accounts of Jesus' life were handled during this lapse of time is the major concern of *form criticism* (which can give rise to theologically conservative or liberal conclusions; generally speaking, liberal theologians have sought to emphasize the length of that intervening period of time). Taking its impetus from rationalism, form criticism emerged after World War I in Germany largely through the influence of two liberal spokesmen. The first spokesman was Martin Dibelius, who set forth his major statement on the topic in *Die Formgeschichte des Evangeliums,*[29] the English translation of which is *From Tradition to Gospel.*[30] The other was Rudolf

Bultmann, who wrote *Die Geschichte der synoptis-chen Tradition*.[31] The English translation, *The History of the Synoptic Tradition*,[32] appeared in 1963.

Dibelius, Bultmann, and many others in their wake, have proposed that, during the period of time between the events and conversations of the ministry of Jesus and their recording in the Gospels, many changes crept into the original stories. Furthermore, they taught that the accounts committed to writing were more a reflection of the immediate social and religious situations of that hour (''Sitz im Leben'') than of the faded setting of Jesus' own life and ministry. In Bultmann's words, ''A literary work or a fragment of tradition is a primary source of the historical tradition out of which it arose, and is only a secondary source for the historical details concerning which it gives information.''[33]

It is certainly sound to conclude that the purposes of the writer and the life situation of his intended audience would influence his selection of material to use. This is something quite other than the conjecture that he would feel the liberty to modify it to suit his ends. Actually, ''form critcism'' is a misnomer when used to describe this liberal view, since the term implies the criticism of the Gospels; yet in reality its major addition to the discussion is a construct of its own. In this sense, liberal criticism is not primarily critical, but creative. It presupposes that the original eyewitness accounts were passed along with varying degrees of unreliability (depending on which critique you read), but generally gathering religious and interpretive baggage in the process. The end result? Many form critics tell us we must be very careful when making any statements about the historical Jesus, if we do so at all.

So it is not unusual to see expressed, hand in hand with theories that late-date the New Testament documents, the assertion that Jesus never claimed deity. In the section that follows, we will see the reason for this partnership: if the documents date early, it is impossible to avoid the conclusion that Jesus claimed deity. Especially is this so if they were written by the persons credited by tradition as the authors, all of whom were eyewitnesses or privy to eyewitness accounts. Of course, conservative theologians, who have held to the doctrine of the inspiration of Scripture, have not been overly concerned if they believed a long period intervened between the events and their recording, since inspiration has been seen as the guarantee of the reliability of these accounts. In contrast, liberal criticism is *critically* dependent on the intervening time for the mutation of the real histories. Is there evidence (apart from the theory itself) that such a gap in time occurred? Is there evidence that it did not?

Recently, there has been an upheaval in the late-date view of the New Testament documents. This author recalls participation in an incident in the early 1960s that well portrays this upheaval. As the director of a student religious group at a private college, I was a member of an interfaith committee of such directors. The late-date view always had the strongest voice within the Christian sector of the committee. As a special project, the eminent William F. Albright, who was the W. W. Spence Professor of Semitic Languages at Johns Hopkins and the dean of biblical archaeologists, gave a lecture series at the campus. However, the committee members who invited him discovered, to their surprise, that Albright's archaeology had forced him to change his view to one at odds with theirs. In his lectures he set forth cogent arguments for early dates for the New Testament documents.

Recent Bombshells

Although set apart by his great stature in the discipline of archaeology, Albright is not alone in this shift. Many others have made similar adjustments of their views. One of the most notable changes among theologians is undoubtedly that of Cambridge theologian John A. T. Robinson (Author of *Honest to God),* whose earlier views are frequently cited in *The Passover Plot.* As a matter of fact, shortly before his death, C. H. Dodd, a theologian of similar liberal inclination, wrote to Robinson that Robinson's change in position on the date of John's Gospel "takes one's breath away. . . ."[34] In his 1976 title, *Redating the New Testament,* Robinson has come out with a more conservative position on the dates of the New Testament books than has been held by most conservative theologians! His shift is sure to send ripples for years to come.

A Sample of Early-date Evidences

Let us look first at the dating of Luke's Gospel. It is the easiest to date because it bears a fixed relationship in time to the book of Acts. Luke, the physician, is the author of Acts; this is attested to by several factors. The book was written by one of Paul's traveling companions. Of these, all but Luke are mentioned in the third person. This would seem to eliminate them, since the writer uses the first person pronoun "we" (Acts 16:10-16). The medical terminology in the book and the high caliber of the Greek are among several further evidences. Also, there are serial salutations in Luke and Acts. Luke 1:3 is addressed to Theophilus, and in Acts 1:1, written by Luke, the author says, "The first account I composed, Theophilus, about all that Jesus began to do and teach. . . ." Thus the book of Acts is the sequel to the Gospel of Luke. We can date the book of Acts with fair certainty, and this, of course, provides an upper limit for the date of Luke.

Acts makes no mention of Paul's death, which may have occurred in A.D. 64, but no later than 67. Such an omission about the central figure of this missionary narrative is extremely difficult to imagine, unless Paul's death had not occurred prior to the completion of Acts. This would place the composition of Acts somewhere between the early and mid-60s.

So we are quite safe in placing Acts somewhere in the early to mid-60s, and Luke before that. Although Luke was not himself an eyewitness to the events of Jesus' ministry, he was an investigative reporter, in the most genuine sense of the term. He begins his Gospel with these words (Luke 1:1-3):

Inasmuch as many have undertaken to compile an account of the things accomplished among us, just as those who from the beginning were eyewitnesses and servants of the Word have handed them down to us, it seemed fitting for me as well, having investigated everything carefully from

the beginning, to write it out for you in consecutive order, 51
most excellent Theophilus.

A Tracer on
the Truth

Here Luke mentions that others have already committed to writing ("compiled an account of") their firsthand observances. He further states that his sources included such eyewitness accounts. This certainly fits the finding of scholarship, since most theologians today, regardless of their theological persuasion, agree that Luke and Matthew are dependent on Mark for much of their information.

In his book, *Rock, Relics and Biblical Reliability,* Clifford Wilson discusses the question posed by some scholars concerning the accuracy of Luke's knowledge about the events he records and the vindication for Luke that came with the discovery of important papyri in the Fayum region of Egypt by Grenfell and Hunt:[35]

> In Luke 2:1-7, the enrollment (census) at Bethlehem is recorded. Scholars had questioned the accuracy of this narrative on four counts:
>
> 1. That a census took place in the reign of Herod, at the decree of Caesar Augustus;
> 2. That everyone had to return to his ancestral home;
> 3. That everyone in the Roman Empire was involved; and
> 4. That Quirinius was then Governor of Syria.
>
> The papyrus documents recovered by Grenfell and Hunt showed that there was a fourteen-year census cycle instituted by Augustus, and that "the Papyri are quite consistent with Luke's statement that this was the first enrollment."[36]

This vindication by archaeology is not unlike a host of other vindications that have commended Luke as a most careful historian. Archaeology has hardly presented Luke as a writer who, years after the events, took bits and snatches of history now encased in accumulated myths and strung them together to serve some purpose immediately at hand. No, the evidence we have about Luke's knowledge and caution is impressive, as is shown by the work of the prestigious archaeologist of the last century, Sir William Ramsay. Ramsay, inspired by the Tübingen School, had concluded that Acts was a second-century work incapable of speaking with authority or accuracy concerning the missionary journeys of Paul and their historical settings. However, as investigation after investigation of the details of Acts bore out its high accuracy, Ramsay reversed his view and finally endorsed Luke as a "historian of the first rank."[37]

The Gospel of Mark

It was once generally held that the material common to the synoptic Gospels had its source in Matthew, which was held to be the earliest of the three, and that Luke and Mark were literarily dependent on Matthew. This view is no longer universally held. Instead, a consensus today agrees that Mark played the primal role as source. As such, we must date it prior to Luke's Gospel, and this pushes the record back still farther, by some number of years. However, before looking at other evidences to seek to narrow the range of acceptable dates, note that the date of the early 60s would qualify Mark as an excellent historical source on the life of Christ. Edwin Yamauchi of Miami University (Ohio) observes: "Even if Mark were to be dated in the 60s, this would not detract from its value. What is of the greatest importance is its claim to eyewitness evidence and firsthand recollections."[38]

Nevertheless, some scholars do not place it in the 60s but, instead, at least as early as the 50s. F. F. Bruce points out that his predecessor at Manchester, T. W. Manson, "was willing to push it back into the 50s considering that a suitable occasion for its publication might have been the reconstitution of the church in Rome about A.D. 55, after its dispersion when Claudius banished the Roman Jews about A.D. 49."[39]

Two questions will concern us as we seek to show what parameters of dating are currently discussed for Mark's Gospel. First, there is the view of some scholars that, since Mark has a veiled reference (Mark 13:14) to the desecration of the temple, and since the reference no doubt relates to the time of Jerusalem's destruction by the Romans under Titus in A.D. 70, Mark must have been composed after this event—or possibly shortly before it, when the course of the near future could be foreseen by the observant eye. This would mean a date of the late 60s or after 70 for Mark's composition.

However, it is fair to question the reasoning process used here. The prediction quoted in Mark 13:14 is made by Jesus. Jesus is seen throughout the historic record as having supernatural powers. Now Jesus' powers (including the prophetic gift) rest on his identity, which is the point finally in question. It is unsound and unfair to use one's *conclusion* about the identity of Jesus in the reasoning process that is supposedly taking one there. Scholars who date Mark on the basis of such a foregone conclusion (that Jesus could not have predicted the future) betray that the conclusion has indeed gone *before*. A more honest approach would be to recognize that Mark 13:14 offers little real help in the dating of the Gospel.

Mark is the "contact man" for Peter's testimony. It is conceded by most that Mark, who is mentioned as Barnabas's traveling companion in the book of Acts (15:39), is also the youth mentioned in Mark 14:51 as an eyewitness to Jesus' arrest. In any case, the writings of the apostolic fathers give uniform testimony that Mark was Peter's assistant and close companion and that Peter was himself the primary source of Mark's information. Opinions differ as to whether Mark served as Peter's secretary, taking down Peter's very words as he dictated them privately, or whether Mark recorded the events as he heard them repeatedly in Peter's public ministry. If the latter were the case, then it is still uncertain whether Mark did so at Peter's request or whether Mark took the initiative to do so himself.

A second issue relating to the date of Mark is the split testimony of church tradition concerning Peter's relationship to this Gospel. Irenaeus records that Mark wrote his Gospel after Peter's death, while Clement of Alexandria says he wrote it before Peter's death. Scholarship is divided as to how this split testimony should be reconciled. One interesting proposal, and certainly a plausible one, is that it was begun while

Peter was alive, but had to be completed after his death.[40]

It has been suggested that 2 Peter 1:15 is Peter's assurance that he would have his extensive firsthand knowledge committed to writing before his death: "And I will also be diligent that at any time after my departure you may be able to call these things to mind." This likely interpretation would favor the view that Mark's Gospel was at least begun, if not actually completed, prior to Peter' death.

Regardless of how we choose between the words of Irenaeus and Clement, it should be clear that Mark is relating to us his intimate knowledge of the accounts of Peter, whose vantage point for observation was second to none, and that Mark likely brought to the task his own eyewitness observances. Undoubtedly, Peter often repeated and clarified his accounts of Jesus' life publicly, and he may well have had extensive notes of his own recorded during Jesus' ministry. Thus, we have reason for the greatest confidence in what was originally written in the Gospel of Mark.

The Gospel of Matthew

The same argument used by some to date Mark shortly before or after A.D. 70 is used with reference to Matthew. In Matthew 22:7 we have a record of Jesus' veiled reference to the destruction of Jerusalem, and in Matthew 24, his open teaching of the future destruction of the temple (verses 1 and 2) and another veiled reference (parallel to Mark 13:14 discussed above) to its desecration. The arguments are no more valid here than they are for Mark's Gospel. Not only so, but throughout his Gospel, Matthew evidences great interest in the fulfillment of prophecy.

It is hard to imagine that he would fail to tell us of the fall of Jerusalem and the destruction of the temple—events that occurred just as Jesus or one of the Old Testament prophets had earlier predicted—had these events already occurred when he wrote. The silence concerning fulfillment of these events, which has long been pointed to by those who date the Gospels early, has now lodged in Robinson's thinking as truly critical. Opening his chapter entitled "The Significance of 70," Robinson says:

> One of the oddest facts about the New Testament is that what on any showing would appear to be the most datable and climactic event of the period—the fall of Jerusalem in AD 70, and with it the collapse of institutional Judaism based on the temple—is never once mentioned as a past fact.[41]

Most theologians date Matthew after Mark, holding that Mark is a literary source for Matthew. It seems reasonable on this basis to date Matthew sometime between the mid-50s and the mid-60s, although some scholars, such as Bruce, date it slightly after A.D. 70. The exact date is not a question of major importance for its soundness, since we have strong evidence from tradition that Matthew, the publican-turned-apostle, is the author. Thus, we add to the testimony of Luke's careful investigative reporting and Peter's firsthand accounts (and possibly some of Mark's) those of Matthew as well.

Matthew was a tax collector by profession. It was to his personal, financial, and political advantage to cultivate habits of meticulous record-keeping prior to joining Jesus' company of disciples. Not only so, but all Jews were acutely conscious of history. Genealogies and written records of important events were undertaken with tenacious care for detail. It would seem reasonable, therefore, that Matthew would have begun extensive notes during or shortly after Jesus' ministry. His testimony is no small addition to the mounting number of reports we have.

Easily the most spectacular of all the rethinking that scholars are doing is that which has resulted in a new-found regard for the Gospel of John. You may have noticed the scarcity of references in chapter two to John's records of Jesus' claims to deity. This is because John's Gospel is full of them, and for that reason (among others) it has long been discounted by many form critics, who have held that John is unreli-

The Gospel of John

able as history. We have sought to make it clear, however, that although John's Gospel is rich in its portrayal of a divine Jesus, it is unnecessary to document such claims. But we will now see that John's Gospel is also early eyewitness testimony and *should not be discounted.*

The John Rylands Papyrus cited earlier anchors the upper limit for the date of John at A.D. 100, give or take a few years. Over the centuries, the majority of scholars had placed it in the 90s of the first century, anyway, and there has been relatively little interest by conservative or liberal scholars in contending over John's date, since the upper limit was fixed. While not contending strongly over its date, conservative scholars often argue for its high historical value, and liberal scholars usually argue against it. However, three lines of evidence have recently led various heretofore skeptical investigators to the conclusion that John dates earlier still and bears the marks of solid history.

The first is a familiar note to you by now. Yes, it is the absolute silence of John's Gospel on the destruction of the temple and Jerusalem in A.D. 70, a fact as inexplicable here as in the Synoptics if they had been written after the event. Robinson goes on to show, in chapter ten of *Redating,* that references to these events "are inescapably present in any Jewish or Christian literature that can with any certainty be dated in the period 70-100."[42] By way of contrast, this underscores the importance of the silence of John and the Synoptics on the subject.

The second reason the Gospel of John is enjoying new recognition is linguistic in nature. John's Gospel has long borne the brunt of criticism by form critics, who have pointed to numbers of figures of speech in John that were representative of the Hellenistic dualism typical in Gnosticism. This dualism, they said, was not found elsewhere in Palestinian literature of the early first century and must have crept into the oral tradition behind John's Gospel during the latter half of the first century and the first part of the second.

What was brought to light with the discovery of the Dead Sea Scrolls, however, is that these dualistic figures had already been in use in Palestine at the time of Christ. They undoubtedly had been implanted, at least in part, from Hellenistic culture. However, they were reinterpreted within Judaism and adopted as useful vessels for Jewish thought. Thus they already constituted a part of the linguistic and conceptual base with which Jesus and his disciples conversed and taught.[43]

Nearly all scholars today agree that the Dead Sea Scrolls are important for dating various New Testament books (although scholars differ as to how important). Albright describes them as highly significant for this reason[44] and states that they give us a linguistic basis for dating the Gospel of John as early as "the late seventies or early eighties."[45] Others, such as Stauffer, are willing to date John even earlier on the same linguistic grounds.

The third and final line of evidence leading scholars to date John earlier is John's rising credibility as one familiar with details of the Palestinian setting as *only an eyewitness would be*. It had long been alleged that John was dependent on the Synoptics for some of his material. This view is taken by Kümmel[46] and Barrett.[47] The number of theologians who reject this view, however, has been growing. In 1938, P. Gardner-Smith argued for John's independence from the Synoptics in *Saint John and the Synoptic Gospels*.[48] C. H. Dodd himself made a contribution of first importance to the discussion with his *Historical Tradition in the Fourth Gospel*.[49] In this work, Dodd elaborated on persuasive evidence for the high historical value of John's Gospel. Norman Geisler points out that in addition to the author's *claim* that he was an eyewitness to the events he reports and his frequent use of first-person references (20:2; 21:4), the author's knowledge of the Jewish customs of purification (2:6), burial (19:40), and feasts (5:1); of Jewish attitudes (7:49); and of the geography and topography of the land (2:12; 4:11; 5:2; 18:11; 19:17) is obviously that of a Palestinian Jew who had been present.[50]

An excellent illustration of John's familiarity with the physical features of Jerusalem is his casual description (John 5:2) of the Pool of Bethesda (also known as the Sheep Pool). Joachim Jeremias points out how the recovery of this pool by archaeologists "presents new and imposing evidence for the reliability of our Gospel tradition in general, but in particular for the validity of local references concerning Jerusalem in the Fourth Gospel."[51] (See Figure 3.) In addition, John was "remarkably well informed about the parties and divisions of Judaism before the Jewish war."[52] George Ladd points out that "many contemporary scholars now recognize a solid Johannine tradition, independent of the Synoptics, stemming from Palestine and dating from A.D. 30-66."[53]

Stauffer has shown how repeated attempts to make John appear out of touch have boomeranged.[54] The view of John's dependence on the Synoptics for his

Figure 3. The sheep pool of Bethesda in Jerusalem. John's Gospel makes casual but knowledgeable reference to it in the present tense.

material is now being dismissed as unnecessary. Indeed, we understand why Robinson refers to "the mass of evidence which in recent years had led to a major revaluation of the historical tradition behind the fourth gospel, reinforcing the conclusion, argued by conservative scholars all along, that it reflects intimate

These evidences favoring John's authorship of the
Gospel bearing his name—the book's remarkable accuracy, the linguistic precedents in Palestine for John's
figures of speech, and the book's silence on the destruction of Jerusalem or her temple—are indeed impressive in magnitude; little by little the school of
skepticism is collapsing.

**The Epistles
of Paul**

One final but major biblical source of early information remains: the various Pauline epistles to the first-.
century churches. These epistles are the earliest of the
New Testament materials providing information on
Christianity and its founder. As a matter of fact, although the *exact* dates of most of the epistles cannot
yet be determined on bases of independent and incon-
testable information, the *range* of dates possible is
fixed as quite narrow. Furthermore, this range, for
most of the epistles, enjoys a secure consensus, un-
challenged by either conservative or liberal scholars
today.

With the book of Acts serving as the historical
guide, scholars work to locate within this frame of
reference the writing of the various epistles. The background data provided by Eusebius, Josephus, Tacitus,
and others, as well as by archaeological workers today,
helps to enrich and authenticate the picture given in
Acts. Occasional points in the historical framework of
Acts can be fixed with accuracy by references to these.
The most notable example of this is the establishment
of the dates of Gallio's proconsulship over Achaia (see
Acts 18:12) through the discovery of an inscription at
Delphi, published in 1905.[56]

The dates of Paul's epistles range from A.D. 50 to
67.[57] Some liberal theologians still maintain that Paul
(who was martyred under Nero in A.D. 67) was not the
true author of Ephesians, 1 and 2 Timothy, or Titus,
which they place from A.D. 80 to after the turn of the
century. It would be gratuitous to grant this point, but
even if we did, we would still have the totality of Paul's

teaching intact. Especially when we come to the person, claims, and ministry of Jesus, these four epistles add nothing to Paul's testimony in Romans, 1 and 2 Corinthians, Galatians, Philippians, Colossians, Philemon, and 1 and 2 Thessalonians—considered genuinely Pauline by all.

What exactly is the significance of these uncontested Pauline epistles? We know they are early writings that enjoyed wide circulation. But Paul was not a eyewitness to Jesus' life and teachings. Is not his teaching therefore hearsay? The answer is that Paul falls into the same category as Luke. That is, Paul knew Peter, James, and John personally (Gal. 1:18, 19; 2:9), and, no doubt, many other eyewitnesses as well. He was privy to these numerous eyewitness sources, inquired carefully of the facts concerning Jesus, and submitted his resulting message to the examination and correction of the apostles (Gal. 2:2, 9).

We do not have to bait Paul to tell us his view of Jesus. Nor, after he has told us, do we have to rush to the dictionary for clarification. Paul tells us in several ways that he thinks Jesus is God. This, like the witnesses of the Gospel writers and James, is the highest kind of evidence that Jesus at least claimed deity. In addition to the implication of a virgin birth made in Galatians 4:4, Paul's teaching on Jesus includes the following:

1. that Jesus was the preexistent Creator of the universe (Col. 1:15-16)
2. that Jesus existed both in the "form of man" and in the "form of God" (Phil. 2:5, 8)
3. that Jesus had been resurrected from the dead, and thereafter was seen by over five hundred eyewitnesses (most of whom were alive when Paul wrote) (1 Cor. 15:4, 5)
4. that prayer could be directed either to God the Father or to Jesus (1 Cor. 1:2)
5. that one day Jesus would return to earth as the divine judge of humanity (2 Thess. 1:7-10)

No first-century Jew—especially one steeped in Jewish orthodoxy as was Paul, trained by the great Rabbi Gamaliel, fiercely monotheistic, a member of the sect of the Pharisees, and possibly even a member of the Great Sanhedrin*—would teach these things about anyone but Jehovah Himself. F. F. Bruce remarks about the correspondence between Paul's picture of Jesus and that presented in the Gospels: "The outline of the gospel story as we can trace it in the writings of Paul agrees with the outline which we find elsewhere in the New Testament, and in the four Gospels in particular."[58]

So Paul's testimony, as one who had access to countless eyewitness sources, is added to the firsthand accounts and investigative reports elaborated on earlier. The harmony of all of the early sources is formidable.

The foregoing summary of evidences is responsible for a veritable cascade of falling dates, as scholars conservative and liberal have reassigned the times when the New Testament reports were written. Concerning archaeology, Albright's statement was bold when published (1955), but is no more:

A New Coalition Emerges

> In general, we can already say emphatically that there is no longer any solid basis for dating any book of the New Testament after about A.D. 80, two full generations before the date between 130 and 150 given by the more radical New Testament critics of today.[59]

In 1963, Albright elaborated:

> Rephrasing the question, I would answer that, in my opinion, every book of the New Testament was written . . . between the forties and the eighties of the first century A.D. (very probably sometime between about 50 and 75 A.D.).[60]

---

*Paul refers to his familiarity with the members of the Sanhedrin in Acts 22:5. His membership in the high court is hinted at in his defense before Agrippa when he refers to voting for the death penalty for Christians prior to his conversion (Acts 26:10). He would have no opportunity for such a vote apart from his membership in that body. It is possible, however, that Paul speaks figuratively here, meaning that he used his informal influence wherever possible to secure the death penalty for the Christians. Nevertheless, Paul's membership in the Sanhedrin remains a good possibility.

The linguistic parallels between the Dead Sea Scrolls and the New Testament have had a powerful influence on theologians, and we can see the emergence of a new coalition of theologians otherwise divided. To names like those cited above—Robinson, Manson, Montgomery, Geisler, Bruce, Stauffer, Kümmel, and Harrison—we could add "many contemporary scholars"[61] or a "majority of scholars"[62] from the right or left with ease.

There is an irony in this emerging coalition. More than one liberal theologian has taught as if the methods of historical research were the exclusive property of liberal theology.[63] Now those theologians, whose scholarship has heretofore gone unquestioned by liberal standards, are arriving at the *same* dates as those who, allegedly, were never considered to have employed sound methods of historical research, *often citing the same reasons.*

Robinson may be correct when he states that "the *span* of time over which the New Testament is thought to have been written has expanded . . . with fashion,"[64] but it can be argued with fair certainty that it was not fashion that caused it to contract. Rather, it was the press of accumulating evidence, in the face of which it is extremely doubtful that the dates will ever again expand. Not long before his death, C. H. Dodd, in his letter to Robinson, penned these pungent words:

> You are certainly justified in questioning the whole structure of the accepted "critical" chronology of the N. T. writings, which avoids putting anything earlier than 70, so that none of them are available for anything like first-generation testimony. I should agree with you that much of this late dating is quite arbitrary, even wanton, the offspring not of any argument that can be presented, but rather of the position of the critic's prejudice that if he appears to assent to the traditional position of the early church he will be thought no better than a stick-in-the-mud.[65]

It would be unfair to present the coalition spoken of above as a monolith that eradicates skepticism; it is certainly not that. Late-date theologians of liberal persuasion were explicit in their theorem that *distance in time* between the occurrence of an event and the recording of that event was a major point against its reliability. The application of this theorem to the New Testament documents, at one time the brainchild of liberal theologians, has turned into a tar baby.

Now that *proximity in time* has been established in the case of the New Testament records, we quite understandably await the inverse conclusion—that this proximity is a strong endorsement of the *reliability* of the documents. Unfortunately, rather than coming forth with such a position, some theologians have put the general public on hold. Others, however, have exhibited a commendable honesty, as they have allowed evidence to exert its proper weight.

> What to an ancient historian is most surprising in the basic assumptions of form-criticism of the extremer sort, is the presumed tempo of the development of the didactic myths—if one may use that term to sum up the matter. We are not unacquainted with this type of writing in ancient historiography, as will shortly appear. The agnostic type of form-criticism would be much more credible if the compilation of the Gospels were much later in time, much more remote from the events themselves, than can be the case.[66]

Most of us, it would seem, will have little difficulty seeing the strength of the arguments for the reliability of the documents. Indeed, some readers may feel that even the sketchy survey presented above is a case of overkill. Nevertheless, the question of the vantage point of the New Testament authors has been a popular query, and it is worthwhile to see something of the mass of evidence that *the reports were indeed written by those who were near to or were actual eyewitnesses of the events they recorded.*

Still another question should be discussed, however, in order to merit a reasoned reliance on the New Testament reports. *Can we count on the integrity of those who have reported to us?* We do well here to remind ourselves that we are especially interested in

Can We Have Confidence in the Integrity of the Witnesses?

their integrity—or lack of it—relative to Jesus' claims to deity. Of course, their general integrity will bear on this specific point, so we will begin there and narrow our focus as we proceed.

Historians are justifiably concerned with the trustworthiness of those whose reports they study. The New Testament writers give evidence of a high sense of integrity, frequently conveying to the reader elements in their reports that reflect quite negatively upon themselves. This is almost unheard of among chroniclers of any sort in any age. Yet it is a repeated feature of the New Testament, as is noticed by Will Durant in his momentous work, *The Story of Civilization*. Durant says of the evangelists:

> They record many incidents that mere inventors would have concealed—the competition of the apostles for high places in the kingdom, their flight after Jesus' arrest, Peter's denial, the failure of Christ to work miracles in Galilee, the references of some auditors to his possible insanity. . . . No one reading these scenes can doubt the reality of the figure behind them.[67]

It is no less important in a court of law to establish the integrity of a witness, for obvious reasons. Irwin Linton, a lawyer, comments on the unabashed artlessness of the Gospels:

> . . . the absence of all parade by the writers about their own integrity, of all anxiety to be believed, or to impress others with a good opinion of themselves or their cause, of all marks of wonder, or of desire to excite astonishment at the greatness of the events they record, and of all appearance of design to exalt their Master. On the contrary, there is apparently the most perfect indifference on their part, whether they are believed or not. It is worthy, too, of special observation, that though the evangelists record the unparalleled sufferings and cruel death of their beloved Lord, and this, too, by hands and with the consenting voices of those on whom he had conferred the greatest benefits, and their own persecutions and dangers, yet they have bestowed no epithets of harshness or even of just censure on the authors of all this wickedness, but have everywhere left the plain and unencumbered narrative to speak for itself, and the reader to pronounce his own sentence of condemnation; like true witnesses, who

It is of note in Durant's comment that the alternative
to honest reporting is invention; not only so, but the
invention of a *conspiracy*. The innocent evolution of a
message is not a plausible explanation of the claim,
because the claim did not come primarily in the form of
a title, or some other third-person reference. It came,
instead, in the form of the first-person theophanic
formula. If it were not authentically Jesus' claim, then
nothing short of deliberate fabrication by his followers
could have attached these words to Jesus' teaching.
Moreover, many and varied sources supply us with the
words and claims of Jesus, and if these be claims
placed on Jesus' lips by others, then it was a carefully
planned and coordinated deception. How plausible is
such a conspiracy?

In the Palestine of the Jews—the capital of
monotheistic religion—such a construct is extremely
unlikely. This is so, first, because truth and honesty
were extolled as virtues by the Jews and their Scriptures. They had a natural repugnance for deception.
However, even if this repugnance had been overcome,
there was also a secondary implication of their relgious
culture. They could well expect that few of their fellow
Jews would *buy* such a contrivance—one that appears
to be an affront to monotheism; and history certainly
bears out such skepticism. How likely is it then, that
they would volunteer to *sell* it, if indeed they knew it to
be false?

No Easy Harmony

In addition, our sources display a curious characteristic for any conspiracy. The stories of conspirators are
notorious for their slick harmony. Any seasoned investigator will tell you he smells something afoul when
eyewitness reports of an occurrence fit too readily.
This author recalls a rather unchemical experiment in a
chemistry class that illustrates the point. The instructor
of the class had a more obvious interest in teaching us
how to think than in teaching us chemistry. Two of us

approached her with a plan to stage a fight in the classroom just prior to the start of class, for the purpose of comparing the written accounts other students would turn in. She agreed to our plan, and the following week we staged our fight. When we were afterwards dismissed from the class by our instructor, the students were convinced they had seen a real fight. The instructor then asked the students to write their accounts, as carefully as possible, of exactly what they had observed.

The results were amazing. Although the reports were all truthful and the events could be reconstructed from the accounts, the apparent *diversity* of the reports was their most conspicuous feature. Turning to the biblical documents, the *absence* of easy harmony in many places is a clear mark of authentic reporting imprinted upon the whole of the New Testament.

Another difficulty with any "conspiracy" view is the teaching of the very one for whom they claimed deity. Jesus had laid the highest stress on absolute truthfulness in dealing with God and man. In the Sermon on the Mount, he had taught that oaths to insure the truthfulness of one's words would be unnecessary if one's "yes" meant yes, and one's "no" meant no (Matt. 5:34-37). Jesus taught the highest standard of personal integrity to his disciples, who in turn laid the highest premium on honesty and forthrightness among the members of the early church (Acts 5:1-11). As F. F. Bruce points out, the continuity extends to Paul as well. The character of Jesus as presented in the Gospels is the same as that presented by Paul in his epistles. The picture of Jesus' integrity is uniform. Jesus' self-denial and service to the needy are cited by both the Gospels and Paul.[69] And when Paul exhorts his readers to be imitators of himself, he justifies his surprising advice with the words "just as I also am of Christ" (1 Cor. 11:1).

Nevertheless, suppose for the sake of argument that the disciples had conspired to deify their dead master. Is it even conceivable that they would have died in defense of their contrivance, in the face of repeated opportunities to recant and live? Much has been said of the logical and psychological impossibility of this. It is rare for a person to pay the supreme price for what he believes, but to pay it for what he knows to be false is insanity requiring the utmost loss of contact with reality. Furthermore, we must bear in mind that they all paid the price through martyrdom and persecution.

Finally, we turn our attention to the statements of two theologians as they bear on Jesus' claims. Stauffer, who is quite open to the question of whether Jesus' followers tampered with his words, draws our attention to a statement of Jesus—one that had to embarrass the disciples. He said, "No one knows . . . the Father except the Son" (Matt. 11:27). In contradistinction to the contemporary practice of turning to the Torah—the Law of Moses—for any knowledge of God, Jesus claimed a completely and utterly private knowledge of God. It was a knowledge that agreed with the God portrayed in the Torah, to be sure, but one that was nevertheless completely independent of it.

Stauffer takes pains to point out the scandalous sound of these words to Jewish ears and the embarrassment they brought to the early Jewish believers who quite naturally desired to commend their master to their fellow Jews:

> Is there a possibility that the saying may have sprung from the pre-Hellenistic, Aramaic-speaking early Christian community? My answer is: No. For no one in the early Jerusalem Christian community, or in any other, would ever have dared to invent such a saying for Jesus. Jesus himself and Jesus alone could have been so bold and so solitary, so free and independent, so absolutistic. Indeed, it is amazing that the members of the early church transmitted this disturbing saying at all. . . .[70]

A second theologian, equally at ease with the "tampering" concept, is James Robinson. Stemming from the influence of C. H. Dodd, liberal theology has taught that the early proclamation of the gospel—the *kerygma*—modified and influenced the facts of the life and ministry of Jesus. Robinson discusses this alleged influence and points out a neglected aspect of the view:

The kind of material which the "kerygmatizing" process would leave *unaltered* is the kind of material which fits best the needs of research based upon the modern view of history and the self. For the kerygmatic interest of the primitive Church would leave unaltered precisely those sayings and scenes in which Jesus made his intention and understanding of existence most apparent to them.[71]

Robinson is saying that, even from the liberal point of view, we can rely on the authenticity, above all, of Jesus' statements of self-disclosure.

We can see from the foregoing that the idea of duplicity on the part of the New Testament reporters has almost nothing to commend it. There is much more reason for confidence in the integrity of their reports than for that of any other ancient literature. We have seen that we have the substantially original form of reports, written by those who witnessed or were near to the events they recorded and whose integrity we can reasonably rely on.

chapter four

The Concurring Opposition

Further tests are made of the validity of the New Testament reports, using sources independent of the New Testament writers and the early Christian community. Hostile, neutral, and sympathetic contemporaries of the first-century biblical writers concur with the record of the New Testament that Jesus claimed deity.

If we were confined to the investigation of the previous chapter, we would have ample reason to know with certainty that Jesus said he was God. But we do have independent means of checking this conclusion as well.

The first independent test of the validity and integrity of the reports that we have discussed is a telltale silence in all contemporary literature concerning the claim of Jesus' deity. There is a complete *absence of rebuttal*. Although much was said to deny his deity, nothing was said to deny that he claimed it. (In fact, the 69 first real threat to the infant Christian church came from the Gnostics who wanted to deny his *humanity!*) Yet the early composition and circulation of the various New Testament books meant that these books were exposed to countless eyewitnesses of Jesus' ministry, not to mention thousands more who had relied on the testimony of such eyewitnesses.

Recently, a 1955 find of papyrus fragments from Cave 7 at Qumran—part of the Dead Sea Scrolls—was tentatively identified by Jose O'Callaghan on paleographic grounds as fragments of Mark's Gospel. Subsequent examination by scholars has not confirmed O'Callaghan's contention. However, in the discussion that was generated, Louis Cassels, UPI correspondent and columnist, rightly pointed out that an early date for Mark (and, of course, for any New Testament document) meant that it

> had to survive the acid test of any journalistic or historical writing—being published at a time when it could be read, criticized, and if inauthentic, denounced by thousands of Jews, Christians, Romans, and Greeks who were living in Palestine at the time of Jesus' ministry. That the early church chose Mark as one of only four Gospels . . . to be preserved for posterity . . . also indicates the people closest to the event—Jesus' original followers—found Mark's report accurate and trustworthy, not myth but true history.[72]

F. F. Bruce points out that the evidence indicates the early Christians took care in distinguishing between Jesus' sayings and their own inferences or judgments (see 1 Cor. 7:12) and could therefore appeal to the firsthand knowledge of their hearers with confidence.[73] This point is recognized by Durant[74] and can hardly be overstated in its importance.

Perhaps an example from our own experience will help to picture the significance of this first-century silence. Suppose that, thirty years after Nixon's presidency ended, a nonfiction bestseller portrayed a thoroughly consistent picture of Nixon having left office before his second term expired for reasons of personal health while at the height of popularity. Is it conceivable that there would be no replies, no hint of public outcry, no suggestion that what was seeking to pass for nonfiction was really a blatant misrepresentation of the facts? Although most of us did not know Nixon personally, we would certainly know enough to contribute to the rebuttal.

In the same way, there can be no doubt that hundreds of eyewitnesses remained alive when the various Gospels and the epistles of Paul were circulating. Harold Hoehner has shown that Jesus' crucifixion was probably in April, A.D. 33.[75] If this date is accepted, those in their teens during the 30s would have been able to recall vividly their observations of this magnetic Jesus many years later. They would be in their late thirties or early forties when Paul's letters began to circulate, and in their late forties or fifties when the Gospel accounts were produced. Moreover, the disciples were young men when they followed Jesus on earth—probably none were over thirty. They and thousands of their generation would be in their early sixties when the Gospels began to circulate, long after Paul's epistles had public exposure (see Figure 4, p. 72).

Demographic studies relating to longevity in the first century A.D. show that hundreds of these eyewitnesses would still be alive in their sixties, and indeed in their seventies and beyond.[76] The Pax Romana promoted long life, on the average, during that era. Life styles in primitive or rural conditions are robust, and, except for specific causes of premature death—such as famine, disease, and war—life expectancies are surprisingly high.[77] It is even likely that some members of the Sanhedrin that tried Jesus, and certainly many of the young understudies of the high court who attended its sessions as observers, would be among those alive at the time the accounts began to circulate.

Just what would be the attitudes of these eyewitnesses toward the Gospels and epistles? It is a common impression of our day that first-century Jews were simple folk, superstitious, and easy prey for whatever magic came their way. However, this is an unwarranted image. (One of the most comfortable prejudices possible is a prejudice toward those of past centuries, since we never will be confronted by those who are its object. Nearly every age has indulged in

Jesus: God,
Ghost
or Guru?

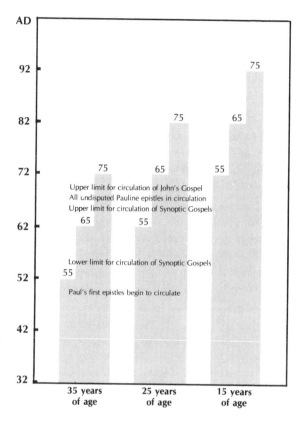

Figure 4. Ages of surviving eyewitnesses to Jesus' life, superimposed on dates for circulation of New Testament documents.

it, and it is often expressed in the phrase "we now know."). The first-century Jews were not gullible. Stauffer talks of their response to miracles:

> This evidence in the sources cannot be discounted psychologically on the ground that in those days all stories of miracles were credulously accepted and uncritically spread about. For the Jews of antiquity were extremely realistic in regard to miracles, and at least the opponents of Jesus among them were highly critical. Had

that not been so, the miracles of Jesus would not have
been so vehemently discussed and so gravely misinterpreted.[78]

However, the Jewish reluctance to accept any claim
of deity for Jesus would go far beyond mere prag-
matism. The Jews' hatred of idolatry rested on the first
of the Ten Commandments, a hatred that by Jesus'
time had become the source of a fierce national pride. It
constituted a wall of disdain between the Jew and
surrounding Gentile nations. This disdain was constantly fueled by the ostentatious Roman presence in
Palestine: the troops in Jerusalem, the Roman governor living in state at Caesarea and the surly tetrarch
Herod and his entourage at Tiberias, all with their
many trappings of idolatry. Had such a claim been
superimposed on Jesus, it would have been regarded as
a repugnant idolatry, and the outcry would have thun-
dered. Nor should we forget that the Sanhedrin's written records[79] of Jesus' trial were probably available
when the accounts were circulating, at least until A.D.
70. Specifically, the synoptic Gospels report on the
Sanhedrin trial (Matt. 26:57-68; Mark 14:53-65; Luke
22:54-71). The Sanhedrin records certainly would
have been produced quickly to deny that Jesus had
claimed deity before that body.

In fact, the Sanhedrin was charged with the responsibility of keeping the people informed of its acts[80] and
may have spoken to the people on the trial of Jesus at its
own initiative. Both Justin Martyr, writing in the second century, and Eusebius[81] mention a circular letter
issued by the Sanhedrin to counter the evidence of the
empty tomb. Justin Martyr quotes directly from it,

. . . a certain Jesus of Galilee, an apostate preacher whom
we crucified; but his disciples stole him by night from the
tomb in which he had been placed after his removal from
the cross; they did this in order to persuade men to
apostasy by saying that he had awakened from the dead
and ascended into heaven.[82]

In point of fact, the Jews still maintained a tradition
of their own a century later, independent of the New
Testament documents.[83] Far from denying that the true

Jesus had feigned no divine character, these traditions confirm, as we shall see later, that this very claim was the reason the Jews rejected Jesus. Furthermore, Matthew, writing sometime between A.D. 65 and 70, said, "And this story has been spread among the Jews to this day" (Matt. 28:15). Thus, even before the Gospels were circulated, the content of their teaching had been circulating, and the easily documented rebuttal would have been provoked to light.

Additional motives to expose such a contrivance existed as well. Each of these motives would have exerted its own substantial press on the actions and responses of people. During the decades in which the accounts first circulated, there were growing hostilities between the Jews and the Romans. The Roman practice of emperor worship took impetus from Augustus (who reigned from 30 B.C. to A.D. 14) and flourished increasingly during those decades. There is ample evidence that the Jewish antipathy for idolatry was a growing irritation to the Romans. It is obvious that this pressure would have increased the desire of orthodox Jews to discredit the Christian worship of Jesus. It is even conceivable that Roman money might have been available as bribes to those who could expose misrepresentations of the reports and thus dispel the worship of Jesus that was so unpopular to all elements of the first-century world.

To further compound the enigma, Paul, writing within thirty years of the events themselves, confidently challenged his readers to check with any eyewitnesses if they wanted to confirm the truthfulness of his message (1 Cor. 15:5)! Yet none of these factors ever moved a single eyewitness to break silence and offer a rebuttal. *The fact that Jesus claimed deity is without a challenger in the first-century historical records.* It seems most unreasonable to ignore this silence.

Independent Confirmation

It may be said—and rightly so—that the foregoing is an argument from silence. It is, however, a vocal silence with a definitive message. But history will go us one better: it affords us the confirmation—in a variety of forms—that Jesus indeed made the claim. This confirmation comes from passive or hostile Greek and Roman historians, hostile Jewish sources, and sympathetic Christian sources.

Greek and Roman Historians. Several voices from the first- and early-second-century world of the Gentiles have survived to provide valuable background information for an investigation of the times. Among them are historians Cornelius Tacitus (ca. A.D. 56-120), Suetonius (ca. A.D. 69-after 122), and Thallus (ca. A.D. 50), whose work survives only in the quotations of others. Their writings provide elaboration on the themes of the New Testament and the life and death of Jesus.

Two other writers—both hostile to Christianity—are worthy of specific mention, since their comments bear directly on the topic of Jesus' claim to deity. First, we have the second-century work of Lucian, a Greek satirist, on the death of Peregrine. In this work Lucian says of Jesus:

> . . . the man who was crucified in Palestine because he introduced this new cult into the world. . . . Furthermore, their first lawgiver persuaded them that they were all brothers one of another after they have transgressed once for all by denying the Greek gods and by worshipping that crucified sophist himself and living under his laws.[84]

Notice that Lucian specifically pins the blame for the worship of Jesus on "their first lawgiver" himself.

A second remark comes from Plinius Secundus (ca. A.D. 61-112), known as Pliny the Younger. As governor of Bithynia, Pliny wrote to the emperor Trajan about the extermination of Christians. He had killed so many, yet so many remained that Pliny sought further direction from Trajan, to whom he elaborates:

> . . . made them curse Christ, which a genuine Christian cannot be induced to do. . . . They affirmed, however, that the whole of their guilt, or their error, was that they were in the habit of meeting on a certain fixed day before it was light, when they sang in alternate verse a hymn to Christ as to a god, and bound themselves to a solemn

oath, not to any wicked deeds, but never to commit any fraud, theft, adultery, never to falsify their word, not to deny a trust when they should be called upon to deliver it up.[85]

Jewish Polemics. From these remarkable testimonies of hostile Gentiles, we turn to extrabiblical Jewish sources. Once more, we find the chorus of witness expanding in perfect harmony with the New Testament contention. As a matter of fact, the Jewish polemics against Jesus that follow are based on Jesus' claim; even their language recalls quite vividly the very words of Jesus as recorded in the Gospels. This is an important agreement, since, as we said earlier, the Jews maintained a tradition about Jesus of Nazareth, independent of the New Testament, well beyond the time frame of these polemics.[86]

The first polemic of note is in the commentary of Rabbi Eleazar Hakkapar (ca. A.D. 170) on the oracles of Balaam (Num. 23:19), provided by the rabbinical school of the Torah at Caesarea:

> God saw that a man, son of a woman, would come forth in the future who would endeavor to make himself God and to lead the whole world astray. Therefore he spoke: "Beware that you do not err by following that man." For it is said: "A man is not God. . . . And if he says he is God, he is a liar. And he will lead men astray and say that he is going and will come back again at the end of days." Is it not so that he spoke thus, but he will not be able to do it.[87]

In a second revealing polemic, Rabbi Abbahu of Caesarea (ca. A.D. 270) puts the words of Jesus into Balaam's mouth:

> If a man says, "I am God," he is a liar; if he says "I am the Son of Man," his end will be such that he will rue it; if he says, "I shall ascend to heaven," will it not be that he will have spoken and will not be able to perform?[88]

It is uncertain exactly how Jesus' claims were preserved in such clarity. It may be, however, that his words before the Sanhedrin were recorded and that these words may have been repeated in the circular letter from the Sanhedrin referred to earlier. It seems plausible that the circular letter would have had a better chance of surviving the Roman invasion in A.D. 70 than would the court records. In the mid-sixties A.D., Paul said to King Agrippa that these things were "not done in a corner," a statement that may have behind it this circular letter. Paul may also have had in mind the circulation of a Logia, or written record of Jesus' sayings used by the Gospels, as well as other sources included in Luke's portfolio (Luke 1:1-2). Nevertheless, the commentaries above reveal that Jesus' words were seized upon by the Jews as prima facie evidence of his infamy and that, to their minds, his words justified his death.

The foregoing Roman, Greek, and Jewish evidence, mark you, is of the weightiest kind we could hope for. Stauffer reminds us:

> For if a confrontation of witnesses yields statements that agree on some points, then these points must represent facts accepted by both sides. This principle certainly holds true if the historical traditions of the two groups of witnesses are independent of each other. But it holds true almost as completely in cases where the traditions intersect. For it is highly significant that the witness for the prosecution admits that the witness for the defense is right on certain points; that he agrees with his opponents about certain common facts.[89]

Sympathetic Sources. Still another source, constituting quite remarkable evidence, is identified by Stauffer as an apocalyptic pamphlet—one written to disclose coming events. It gives extremely early confirmation of Jesus' use of the theophanic *ani hu.* Later incorporated into the *Ascension of Isaiah,* the pamphlet was written in approximately A.D. 68[90] as a warning of the atrocities of Nero:

> After it is consummated, Beliar the great ruler, king of this world, will descend . . . in likeness of a man, a lawless king, the slayer of his mother. . . . This king will persecute the plant which the Twelve Apostles of the Beloved have planted. Of the Twelve one will be delivered into his hands. . . . And all that he hath desired he will do in the world; *he will do and speak like the Beloved and he will say: "I am God and before me no god was formed* [italics mine]." . . . And all the people in the

world will believe him. And they will sacrifice to him and they will serve him, saying: "This is God and beside him there is none other." And the greater number of those who shall have been associated together in order to receive the Beloved will turn aside after him. And he will set up his image before him in every city.[91]

Note that the writer states that Nero will claim deity just as did the Beloved (Jesus). He goes on to describe the claim in the language of Psalm 43:10, "I am God and before me no god was formed." As we pointed out in chapter two, phrases similar to this alternate throughout the psalm with *Ani hu* and help to form the clear meaning of Jesus as he employed the theophanic phrase.

We are hardly confronted with a toss-up. The evidences in favor of early, reliable, eyewitness testimony—interlocked with hundreds of cross references that confirm each other—have to be impressive. It is not surprising that Will Durant says:

> In the enthusiasm of its discoveries the Higher Criticism has applied to the New Testament tests of authenticity so severe that by them a hundred ancient worthies—e.g., Hammurabi, David, Socrates—would fade into legend.[92]

These words echo those of the eminent Jewish scholar J. Klausner, who said, "If we had ancient sources like those in the Gospels for the history of Alexander or Caesar, we should not cast any doubt upon them whatsoever."[93] Nevertheless, those concerned with the question are the surer now, having sought out, followed, and survived the paths of skepticism.

Options: Open and Obsolete

We have seen—through many reliable windows into the first century—that Jesus made the supreme claim for himself. We have observed his behavior, researched his choice of words, blushed with his contemporaries, and watched in amazement as he pushed aside the primacy of his own teaching in religious matters—teaching we would have gladly embraced—to retain the center stage himself. His central prominence is overlooked or impossible to many modern conceptions of Jesus; and the modern alternatives conceived are impossible to harmonize with the Jesus we have seen.

The Moslem faith has a high regard for Jesus as a prophet.[94] This idea has found much comfort in the English-speaking world as well. It is remarkable that many—even among the humanists—are glad to treat Jesus as a sort of Western guru. In this view, we see a happy agreement of humanist and theologian. Termed in *An Encyclopedia of Religion* as the "purely historical view," it explains "that Jesus was either a prophet or a chasid (i.e., a saint or holy man)."[95] However, this position was possible only when it could be said he never alluded to his deity.

I am told that, in spite of newer electronic tuning equipment, the most accurate way to tune a piano is still with a tuning or C-fork. The procedure is to "set the temperament," tuning middle C and then the other Cs up and down the keyboard. Once this is done, the other tones are brought into harmony as the craftsman tunes the "peers." The more skillful the piano tuner, the more completely the outcome depends upon the fidelity of his tuning fork. Occasionally his tuning fork can go off pitch and, when it does, failure to replace it can result in a piano that is internally consistent, but completely off-key.

Just as with a tuning fork, a starting premise can be in error, and yet everything that follows may be "tuned" to a flawless internal consistency. In the case at hand, the starting premise for years has been that Jesus never murmured a word about his own deity. But, confronted with the claim, this old tuning fork must be discarded, causing a great narrowing of the choices now possible.

From his claims it follows quite logically that Jesus cannot be a prophet, a great teacher, or a holy man. These, and a host of other concepts are eliminated. Because Jesus was a Jew who upheld the Great Shema of Israel—the confession "The Lord our God is one!" (Deut. 6:4)—and the many injunctions against the worship of idols in the Torah, there is no way to read pantheism into his remarks. He did not claim to be God in some pantheistic sense that was also true of the Pharisee.

The simple fact is that only three possibilities remain. C. S. Lewis was probably not the first to post this "trilemma." (It is one of those irreducible pieces of logic that is so evident that no one, especially a Lewis, would bicker over its origin.) But Lewis doubtless expressed it best:

> I am trying here to prevent anyone saying the really foolish thing that people often say about Him: "I'm ready to accept Jesus as a great moral teacher, but I don't accept His claim to be God." That is the one thing we must not say. A man who was merely a man and said the sort of things Jesus said would not be a great moral teacher. He would either be a lunatic—on a level with the man who says he is a poached egg—or else he would be the Devil of Hell. You must make your choice. Either this man was, and is, the Son of God: or else a madman or something worse. You can shut Him up for a fool, you can spit at Him and kill Him as a demon; or you can fall at His feet and call Him Lord and God. But let us not come with any patronising nonsense about His being a great human teacher. He has not left that open to us. He did not intend to.[96]

In the chapters that follow, we will explore these alternatives. Was Jesus a liar? Was he mentally deranged? We will give legitimate consideration to these questions.

chapter five

Master of
the Big Lie?

The possibility is considered that a purely human Jesus, in full possession of his mental capacities, merely lied about his identity. The evaluation of this hypothesis includes a discussion of motive and opportunity, as well as relevant sociological and psychological factors.

Durant refers to the life and moral character of Jesus as "the most fascinating feature in the history of Western Man."[97] Was he a liar? Could he have set out to deceive his family and disciples and have been successful? Is it possible that this man, whose moral teachings are on the lips of millions twenty centuries later, pulled off the coup d'etat of all time? At the outset, we have to face it: if Jesus lied, he is the *master* of the big lie. No bolder idea could be conceived, no lie more surely destined to collapse. It is noteworthy that this option has never gained much popularity. It is beleaguered by many serious problems.

The first problem, of course, is the evidence of Jesus' own moral brilliance, evidence that has inspired even the most skeptical to extol his life as exemplary. This response, dating from our time back to his earliest followers, is entirely consistent with his own view of himself. We see this most clearly in contrast:

> On the one side clear, definite moral teaching. On the other claims which, if not true, are those of a mega-lomaniac, compared with whom Hitler was the most sane and humble of men. There is no half-way house and there is no parallel in other religions. If you had gone to Buddha and asked him "Are you the son of Bramah?" he would have said, "My son, you are still in the vale of illusion." If you had gone to Socrates and asked, "Are you Zeus?" he would have laughed at you. If you had gone to Mohammed and asked, "Are you Allah?" he would first have rent his clothes and then cut your head off. If you had asked Confucius, "Are you Heaven?" I think he would have probably replied, "Remarks which are not in accordance with nature are in bad taste."[98]

But Jesus said, *"I am . . . the truth"* (John 14:6). This was no ad lib, no mere figure of speech, selected at random to impress his followers. Jesus gave every evidence, as we discussed earlier, of great concern for the importance of truthtelling, yet always with a wonderful gentleness (John 4:17-18).W. E. H. Lecky, the esteemed British historian of the nineteenth century (and, incidently, not a believer), described Jesus' character in his *History of European Morals from Augustus to Charlemagne:*

> The character of Jesus has not only been the highest pattern of virtue, but the strongest incentive to its practice, and has exerted so deep an influence, that it may be truly said, that the simple record of three short years of active life has done more to regenerate and to soften mankind, than all the disquisitions of philosophers and than all the exhortations of moralists.[99]

We have earlier discussed the consistency between Jesus' own highly ethical and moral life and teachings and indicated how these extended to the lives and teachings of the New Testament writers and to the early church of which they spoke. Indeed, the pages of the New Testament are laced with the highest tributes to truthfulness, honesty, and moral wholeness. And when the writers of the New Testament were faced with incidents that reflected their own frailty or that of their fellow believers, they did not compound these incidents by denying them or covering them up. Jesus' own moral integrity emanates in concentric circles from his life to his teaching, from there to his disciples' lives and to their teaching, on to the early church, and from there outward in a thousand byways of history. This bright influence on the dusky stage of history was so great that R. R. Palmer exclaimed:

> It is impossible to exaggerate the importance of the coming of Christianity. It brought with it, for one thing, an altogether new sense of human life. For the Greeks had shown man his mind; but the Christians showed him his soul. They taught that in the sight of God all souls were equal, that every human life was sacrosanct and inviolate. Where the Greeks had identified the beautiful and the good, had thought ugliness to be bad, had shrunk from disease and imperfection and from everything misshapen, horrible and repulsive, the Christian sought out the diseased, the crippled, the mutilated, to give them help. Love for the ancient Greek was never quite distinguished from Venus. For the Christians who held that God was love, it took on deep overtones of sacrifice and compassion.[100]

Was it all a piece of theater? If so, we have to greatly admire Jesus the actor. As Kitchener, of the Ontario *Daily Record,* said, "When you try to make an impression, that's the impression you make."[101]

A Hypocrite Too?

Jesus' own moral character is an evidence in its own right. Since he taught the importance of honesty, he would be a hypocrite as well, if he were first a liar. But Jesus exhibits very poor technique for a hypocrite. Instead of sneaking around, smuggling the secrets of his personal life past his generation, he makes the Sadducees and Pharisees so angry with him that they can hardly think of anything else. Then he challenges, "Which one of you convicts me of sin?" (John 8:46).

That is a formidable invitation to give even one's friends, let alone one's enemies. Those are strange words for a man who has something to hide. Furthermore, Jesus explicitly holds up his integrity as evidence of his identity. For a liar, that would be something like a novice demanding that the net be removed so that he can demonstrate that he is a master tightrope walker.

Worse still, *if* Jesus was not God and knew it, he would have been a vile and heinous person, because he went around teaching his followers to suffer persecution for his name's sake (Matt. 5:11-12). What a vast and needless treachery! Nietzsche would have been right—Jesus, the champion of humility and patient suffering—*would* be the culprit of history! Turning the other cheek should be classed with feudalism and scholasticism and driven from the planet!

Furthermore, Jesus taught that he was to sit in judgment on mankind in the last days and that the personal response of others to the very claim in question would be the basis for their judgment (Matt. 7:21-24; Mark 14:62). If he was a liar, Jesus certainly ranks with the all-time felons!

Moreover, we must realize that Palestine was a terrible place for one to perpetrate the grand deception that he is God. In the well-advertised book *The Myth of God Incarnate*, theologian Maurice Wiles argues that the story found easy reception because the Jewish religion inclined the Hebrew mind strongly in that direction:

> It was within the context of such a general belief in divine intervention that belief in the specific form of divine intervention which we know as the incarnation grew up.[102]

However, this reasoning entirely misses the point that popular belief of Jesus' day was receptive to only particular kinds of revelation. The average Jew could see in his Scriptures a Messiah who would throw off the Roman yoke, but not a "suffering servant." He could see a human Messiah, for so the Son of David was to him, but he had no expectation at all of a

Messiah who was divine, even though such is taught in the Old Testament (see Appendix). The overwhelming tendency of the Jews at that time was to stress the transcendence and remoteness of Jehovah. To say that the Jews were open to incarnation as a category of divine intervention is like saying that modern man is open to snake-oil remedies as a legitimate category of medical science. The latter is no less notorious to modern man than was the former to the ancient Jew, who was likely to associate such claims with the fraudulent idolatries of the Gentiles.

Jesus knew all of this. He also knew that he could have traveled 120 miles to the north, east, or south and found a much readier ear for such a message. One would question the intelligence of a man who selects Palestine for his stage when his act is the impersonation of Jehovah!

The Undeniable Action of Jesus

Still, the strongest argument for rejecting the big lie option is what Jesus *did* and what he *said*. In our day of pluralistic moral approaches, we may reason that talk is cheap. And so it is. And if we grant that in Jesus' day it was even cheaper (which it wasn't), we still cannot make light of Jesus' final behavior. *He volunteered for the cross to punctuate his claim!* What possible motive would an imposter have had for *that?* What gain, what enjoyment of recognition could a liar have anticipated to follow his death? A thoroughgoing materialist would have expected only annihilation after the cross; a Sadducee, the same; a Pharisee, certainly no reward for his lie; and an Essene, a place of infamy in the golden age that was to come.

Yet Jesus' journey to Jerusalem for his final Passover week was resolute, in spite of the warning and pleading of friends. His exposure to his enemies in the Garden of Gethsemane on the eve of his trial was deliberately reckless, and his only defense before the Sanhedrin was a defiant refusal to abandon his claim. No, he did not stumble into the death sentence.

If we wish to view him as a liar, we must realize we are also confronted with a *fool*. Yet a mere man who pulled off the deception Jesus did would have to have immense cunning and prowess. Hypocrisy is no easy pastime, mind you. Jesus played the role of a fulfiller of prophecy before an audience who searched the Law and Prophets intensively. He could not have manipulated the fulfillment of a single prophecy without the most elaborate engineering. Could we expect this shrewd man to be the same one who paid the supreme price for his cheap talk? It is absurd to contemplate in one Jesus the master and the fool.

For these reasons, the big-lie option has never overcome its initial inertia. The vast majority of those who have given thoughtful consideration to the question of Jesus have rejected this as a serious possibility.

chapter six

Delusions or Grandeur?

Consideration is given to the possibility that Jesus was deluded about his identity. Records of his behavior, personality, and relationships are viewed to see if symptoms of psychiatric disorders in which delusions occur were manifested.

Today we have a new romance with Don Quixote. The theater and cinema portray the marriage of the brilliant and the psychotic. Perhaps, we may say, Jesus was some kind of benign lunatic, having his own keen touch with moral brilliance, but having little touch with anything else in the real world. In this chapter, we will examine the mental health of Jesus.

Our approach will be to give the psychiatric descriptions of what a lunatic is: to describe how a mentally ill person feels, thinks, speaks, behaves, and relates to others, and then to evaluate the extent to which Jesus fits that picture from our knowledge of him. We will   87 then seek to describe mental health and to compare the psychological make-up of Jesus with its characteristics.

The key psychiatric symptom of importance to this discussion is that of delusion. If Jesus were deluded, then contact with reality would be impaired, and he could be justifiably described as mentally ill or a lunatic.

It is a cardinal principle, not only in psychiatry but in all of medicine, that whereas one symptom may help to formulate a provisional diagnosis, no final diagnosis should ever be made until additional supportive evidence is revealed. If Jesus' beliefs about his deity were delusional, we should find a constellation of other symptoms to confirm that he was mentally ill. If we are unable to find this contributory information, we should rule out the possibility that he was mentally ill or that he had delusions.

In the case of Jesus, let us first consider the possibility of other evidence before evaluating the matter of delusion itself.

There are four basic psychiatric categories in which delusions may be a symptom. They are:

1. the psychoses associated with organic brain syndromes
2. the major affective disorders
3. schizophrenia
4. paranoia

A brief description of each of these is given in turn.

**Psychoses
Associated
With Organic
Brain Syndromes**

An organic brain syndrome is a disorder, often causing a psychosis, that is itself caused by or associated with actual physical damage to brain tissue. This damage could be caused by any of the following etiologic agents:

1. intracranial or systemic infection (viral, bacterial, or syphilitic)
2. drug or poison intoxication (including alcohol)
3. traumatic, externally induced injury
4. disturbances in blood circulation
5. endocrine, metabolic, or nutritional imbalances

6. epilepsy
7. intracranial tumor (malignant or nonmalignant)
8. degenerative diseases of the central nervous system such as multiple sclerosis and senile atrophy

The basic clinical picture of *organic brain disease* is that of a person experiencing 1) memory loss, especially for recent events; 2) impairment of perceptual responses and of orientation with respect to time, place, and person; 3) disordered and slowed intellectual functioning; 4) faulty judgment; and 5) flatness and instability of emotions leading to an observable change of character, often causing social embarrassment.

According to the *Psychiatric Glossary* of the American Psychiatric Association, a psychosis is:

> a major mental disorder of organic or emotional origin in which the individual's ability to think, respond emotionally, remember, communicate, interpret reality and behave appropriately is sufficiently impaired so as to interfere grossly with his capacity to meet the ordinary demands of life. It is often characterized by regressive behavior, inappropriate mood, diminished impulse control, and such abnormal mental content as delusions and hallucinations.[103]

Involutional melancholia is primarily a depressive mood agitated by menopause. It is most common in women between forty-five and fifty-five, but also occasionally appears in men between fifty and sixty-five. The depression is closely associated with delusional feelings of guilt such as believing that one has committed the unpardonable sin. Suicide is common.

The Major Affective Disorders

Manic depressive illness is a psychosis with *intermittent periods of elation or euphoria alternating with deep depression.* The mood swings are caused by some biochemical imbalance mechanism (as yet only partially identified) that affects the central nervous system, causing uncontrollable high and low emotions.

Hereditary in origin, the high moods can lead to grossly inappropriate behavior, distressing to family and friends; whereas the depressive phases, with their accompanying suicidal thoughts, cause great pain to the patient himself. At both extremes delusions and hallucinations frequently occur.

Schizophrenia

Schizophrenia is the so-called split-personality disease. Actually, the split is not in the personality structure at all, but rather describes the discrepancy between *thinking* and *feeling*. The way a person with schizophrenia perceives a situation emotionally is inappropriate to the reality of the situation. This discrepancy leads to an inability to face up to and deal with reality, the real world outside. It is, therefore, a form of escape from the responsibility of coping with the pressures of the environment by recoil into a protective fantasy world of one's own.

The primary symptoms are: 1) inappropriateness or lack of emotional display to others, leading to protective withdrawal; 2) inability to retain attention to one train of thought; 3) extreme selfishness and self-centeredness in most thoughts, speech, and actions, leading to loss of friends or enjoyment of life; and 4) the inability to hold firm opinions, make definite decisions, or act on them. Secondary symptoms such as delusions, hallucinations, and self-referential ideas occur when the disorder progresses to psychosis.

There are many different types of schizophrenia, the classification being based on which of the foregoing symptoms are the most prominent. Schizophrenia is caused by a combination of factors: genetic predisposition (hereditary factor); metabolism, allergy, or infectious disorder (biochemical factor); and childhood environmental stress with emotional deprivation (social factor).

The Search for Symptoms

Now that three of the four psychiatric categories have been defined, let us turn our consideration to the question, To what extent, if any, did Jesus display the psychiatric symptoms associated with these three categories? Although there is some overlap, the symptoms from these categories of mental illness can be classified into three major groups:

1. gross inadequacy in relating to reality
   a. memory loss
   b. impairment of perceptual responses
   c. faulty judgment
   d. depression alternating with elation
   e. hallucinations (when advanced to the psychotic stage)
   f. loss of reality contact
2. gross inadequacy in interpersonal relationships
   a. flatness and instability of emotions
   b. guilt
   c. self-reference (when advanced to the psychotic stage)
3. gross inadequacy in communication
   a. disordered and slowed intellectual functioning
   b. lack of emotional display toward others
   c. inability to retain attention
   d. inability to hold firm opinions and to make decisions

Did Jesus display difficulty in relating to reality? At the age of twelve Jesus was found "in the temple, sitting in the midst of the teachers, both listening to them, and asking them questions. And all who heard Him were amazed at His understanding and His answers" (Luke 2:46-47). The chapter ends with a one-verse summary of his adolescence and early adulthood: "And Jesus kept increasing in wisdom and stature, and in favor with God and men" (Luke 2:52). It seems as if Jesus had a very happy and secure home and upbringing. This fact alone would have been a major preventative of mental illness in his later life.

In dealing with opposition, Jesus was capable of quick and skillful thinking. When challenged by religious leaders about his source of authority, he said he would tell them only if they first would tell him if the baptism of the popular baptizer, John, was from heaven or of men. Jesus knew that the onlookers of the populace would be incited and alienated if the chief priests, scribes, and elders replied, "Of men." On the other hand, John's endorsement of Jesus meant they could not concede it to be from heaven without increasing Jesus' popularity as a result. Mark describes their response to this insoluble dilemma:

> If we say, "From heaven," He will say, "Then why did you not believe him?" But shall we say, "From men"?—they were afraid of the multitude, for all considered John to have been a prophet indeed (Mark 11:31-32).

Matthew relates that on another occasion the Pharisees "took counsel how they might trip Him in what He said." They tried to trip him with a question about the legality of paying taxes to Rome, playing on the tense political atmosphere of the day. "But Jesus perceived their malice" and told them to pay their taxes to Caesar and their tithes to God. "And hearing this, they marveled, and leaving Him, they went away" (Matt. 22:15, 18, 22).

The incident of Jesus' cleansing of the temple, thought by some to be impulsive, uncontrolled, and irrational behavior, was actually fully controlled and deliberate. It was the product of Jesus' high sense of moral propriety and represented justifiable righteous indignation: "And He made a scourge of cords, and drove them all out of the temple . . . and He poured out the coins of the moneychangers, and overturned their tables" (John 2:15). He was purging from the place of worship the corrupt merchants, who were pretending to be devout religious appointees: "It is written, 'And My house shall be a house of prayer,' but you have made it a robbers' den'" (Luke 19:46). Throughout the foregoing discussion we have seen in Jesus, not a loss of reality contact, but rather a strong grip on the (often distasteful) realities of his world.

Was Jesus inept in relating to others? Unlike the psychotic, who is characterized by social withdrawal, Jesus was very much *involved with people.* He was able to relate on a deep personal level with men and women from all strata of society. Nicodemus, a ruler of the Jews, had a long conversation with Jesus (John 3:1-21), and as a result he became first a supporter and eventually a follower of Jesus (John 7:50-51; 19:39). A Roman centurion (an officer equivalent in rank to a major or lieutenant colonel) came to Jesus for help. His faith was commended and his servant was healed (Mark 8:5-13).

By contrast Jesus was also able to relate to the lowest of society. A woman of low reputation was converted and led others to faith (John 4:6-42); a leper worshiped him and was cleansed (Mark 8:1-4); the despised tax collector Zaccheus, rich but socially ostracized, joyfully entertained Jesus in his home (Luke 19:1-10). The New Testament picture of Jesus is one of a person who enjoyed people and interacted with ease at the level of their needs.

Did Jesus display difficulty in other forms of communication? Unlike the mentally ill person, Jesus was also able to relate to groups and crowds:

> And Jesus was going about all the cities and villages, teaching in their synagogues, and proclaiming the gospel of the kingdom, and healing every kind of disease and every kind of sickness. And seeing the multitudes, He felt compassion for them, because they were distressed and downcast like sheep without a shepherd (Matt. 9:35-36).

During his three-year teaching ministry, "the multitudes were amazed at His teaching; for He was teaching them as one having authority, and not as their scribes" (Matt. 7:28-29). Furthermore, John records that when Jesus spoke about the coming of the Holy Spirit, "some of the multitude therefore . . . were saying, 'This certainly is the Prophet.' Others were saying, 'This is the Christ.' " Officers sent by the chief priests to arrest him returned without him, remarking "Never did a man speak the way this man speaks" (John 7:40-41, 46).

Jesus' social withdrawal is described only three times in the Gospels, none of them for the negative purpose of avoiding people. They were for positive purposes; he withdrew 1) to be with his disciples, 2) to rest and be refreshed (Mark 7:31), and 3) to be alone for prayer (Mark 1:35; Luke 6:12).

Mentally ill people usually collapse when under

great emotional stress. They "decompensate" or lose their contact with reality. By contrast, *under the extreme stresses of his last hours, Jesus remained unbelievably calm and controlled.* The anguish of the Garden of Gethsemane, the violent arrest, the protracted illegal trials, the scourging, the blood loss and dehydration, the lack of sleep throughout the hot night, the rejection by the people, the desertion of his own followers, and the total lack of understanding of his message by virtually everyone would have driven most people to protective psychosis (an emotional withdrawal, causing a person to be unaware of circumstances happening around him). While actually hanging in agony and partial asphyxiation on the cross, his statement "Father, forgive them; for they do not know what they are doing" (Luke 23:34) is the most compelling evidence of his emotional control, contact with reality, and unselfish love.

No, it was not Jesus who cracked under the strain of those hours. It was Peter (John 18:10), trying to deal with the situation by using his sword and ultimately denying his Lord (Mark 26:74). It was Pilate's wife, who had a nightmare (Mark 27:19). It was these and others around him, not Jesus, who crumbled.

In searching through the Gospels, we find no evidence that Jesus had any organic brain disease, manic depressive illness (uncontrollable high or low mood swings), or any of the primary symptoms of schizophrenia. The contrary is actually the case. It turns out that a search for examples of the symptoms that should accompany mental disorder is a long and unrewarding task.

Paranoia

We come next to paranoia, the condition in which delusions are preeminently seen. A delusion is a persistent false belief not in keeping with a person's cultural and educational background or level of knowledge. Both cause and characteristics of delusion provide a basis for identifying it in an individual. As to cause, the belief is usually a result of unmet needs of which the individual is not aware and is maintained in spite of all logical argument and objective contrary evidence.

Characteristically the vast majority of delusions are one of these types: of grandeur, exaggerated ideas of one's importance or identity; of persecution, ideas that one has been singled out for some harm or punishment; or of self-reference, the erroneous assumption that unrelated happenings, behavior, or speech of others applies to oneself. While a *delusion* is a wrong subjective idea or concept about something that does not exist, *illusion* is a perceptual disorder in which something that objectively does exist is misinterpreted. *Hallucinations* are false sensory perceptions in the absence of actual external stimuli. They may be visual (seeing things) or auditory (hearing voices).

Let us first ask if we see in Jesus' life the expected *cause* of delusion. Our description of delusion said, "The (false) belief is usually a result of unmet needs of which the individual is not aware." There is no evidence anywhere in the New Testament that Jesus had unmet unconscious needs. (He had unmet *conscious* needs: "The Son of Man has nowhere to lay His head" [Matt. 8:20].) Whereas unmet conscious needs can be weathered with commensurate courage, unmet unconscious needs usually lead to the development of such neurotic symptoms as depression and anxiety. Far from having these, Jesus showed by his devotion to meeting the needs of others the unusual liberty he had with reference to his own.

Do we see in Jesus' life evidences of the *characteristics* of delusions of grandeur, persecution, or self-reference? With regard to grandeur, Jesus' belief that he was divine does not at all fit the picture of a psychotic with a grandiose delusion. For one thing, Jesus was humble, a characteristic totally at variance with the attitude of paranoid grandeur. Such attitudes are generated from deep feelings of inadequacy and inferiority and are a form of defense mechanism that seeks to compensate for these feelings. But Jesus welcomed little children that the disciples had tried to reject (Matt. 19:14); he washed his disciples' feet (John 13:5); and he prepared breakfast for them when they had become exhausted from a fruitless night of fishing

(John 21:12-13).

Furthermore, Jesus stated very plainly, unlike the grandiose delusional person would do, that it was not he himself who was great, but his Father in heaven. He claimed to be under orders from above: "For I did not speak on my own initiative, but the Father Himself who sent Me has given Me commandment, what to say, and what to speak" (John 12:49). "As the Father gave Me commandment, even so I do" (John 14:31).

Finally, had Jesus been suffering from a grandiose delusion, he would have been too proud to associate with, let alone speak with, such down-and-outers as the woman taken in adultery (John 3:3-11), tax collectors and sinners (Luke 5:27-32), and lepers (Luke 5:12-13). Yet we see, in these conversations and others, a man of warm and solicitous concern.

With regard to persecution and self-reference, Jesus was *in reality* aware that his life was in danger. His lengthy dialogue with doubters and enemies—recorded in John 8—indicated that he knew that he was the center of hot controversy and was cognizant of plots against him. "You seek to kill Me, because My word has no place in you" (John 8:37). Much history, including the previously mentioned Jewish polemics, indicates that these were no delusions. He knew his enemies were *in reality* out to get him, which, of course, they finally did.

"Delusions," as stated previously, "are preeminently seen in the condition of paranoia." The Greek word *paranoia* simply means an abnormal mind. Today it is used specifically to describe someone's behavior or attitude if he is *unrealistically suspicious, jealous, hostile, wary, sensitive, or accusatory*. The *Psychiatric Glossary* defines paranoia as:

> an extremely rare condition characterized by the gradual development of an intricate, complex and elaborate paranoid system of thinking based on (and often proceeding logically from) misinterpretation of an actual event. Frequently the individual considers himself endowed with unique and superior ability. In spite of a chronic course, this condition does not seem to interfere with the rest of the individual's thinking and personality.[104]

True paranoia is manifested by an internally consistent and logical delusional system of beliefs. This system is compartmentalized and separated from the rest of his conscious activity. It is not bizarre or impossible and may contain an element of truth. Absence of schizophrenic symptoms (gross inadequacy in communication, interpersonal relationships, and relating to reality) distinguishes true paranoia from paranoid schizophrenia. However, a true paranoiac, in addition to his false belief system, will usually manifest other less severe evidence of loss of reality contact.

The ego-defense mechanism used is projection—the transfer or attribution of one's own undesirable thoughts or impulses to another person when one is unwilling or unable to admit them as his own. Projection is very often a consequence of insecurity and emotional rejection in early life. Delusions of grandeur, persecution, or self-reference are almost always present and, in extreme cases, could lead to violence toward others. Hallucinations, though not characteristic, sometimes occur.

There were three "actual events" Jesus could potentially have misinterpreted: his birth, his baptism, and the Transfiguration. Yet Jesus' interpretations where shared ones. These were not simply his own ideas. The just and devout Simeon holding the baby Jesus in his arms in the temple said, "For mine eyes have seen Thy salvation" (Luke 2:30). Jesus saw his birth as the literal fulfillment of prophetic writings: "Therefore the Lord Himself will give you a sign: Behold, a virgin will be with child and bear a son, and she will call His name Immanuel [i.e., God is with us]" (Isaiah 7:14). "And gathering together all the chief priests and scribes of the people, he began to inquire of them where the Christ was to be born. And they said to him, 'In Bethlehem of Judea, for so it has been written by the prophet' " (Matt. 2:4-5). The first two chapters of both Matthew's and Luke's Gospels most fully describe this part of his life story.

In paranoiac conditions, "frequently the individual considers himself endowed with unique or superior ability." Such consideration was undoubtedly justified in Jesus' case. Jesus "cried out with a loud voice, 'Lazarus, come forth!' He who had died came forth, bound hand and foot with wrappings" (John 11:43-44). Of course, it is easy to conclude that anyone who believes he can do miracles has a delusion of superior or even supernatural ability. However, such a person is not easily dismissed if sober onlookers are convinced as well. Furthermore, even Jesus' avowed enemies *did not deny his miracles*.[105] No one on the scene did. The denial of his miracles did not come until centuries later.

"Hallucinations, though not characteristic, sometimes occur" in paranoia. In the matter of his baptism by John, the King James Version states: "And Jesus when he was baptized, went up straightway out of the water; and lo, the heavens were opened unto him, and he saw the Spirit of God descending like a dove, and lighting upon him; and lo a voice from heaven, saying, This is my beloved Son, in whom I am well pleased" (Matt. 3:16-17).

This description could easily be of a purely subjective experience and we could therefore interpret the experience as a combined visual and auditory hallucination. However, the more modern and more accurate New English Bible states in part that "at that moment heaven opened . . . and a voice from heaven was heard. . . ." This implies that the event was witnessed by others present and was not, therefore, a private, internal psychological experience on Jesus' part.

In the case of the Transfiguration, the same words were spoken: "This is My beloved Son, with whom I am well-pleased; hear Him!" (Matt. 17:5). On this occasion, however, three other people—Peter, James, and John—were mentioned as present and hearing the words: "And when the disciples heard this, they fell on their faces and were much afraid" (Matt. 17:6). Again, this experience was not subjective nor hallucinatory. Thus far, we have no supportable basis for dismissing such an event as a fabrication, either intentional or unintentional.

In summary, any contention that Jesus was paranoid

or delusional simply does not fit in with present-day descriptions of such psychiatric disorders. The above evidences from the gospel record, though far from complete, are sufficient to document that Jesus' patterns of thought, speech, behavior, and interpersonal relationships were not those of known patterns in people who are mentally ill.

Therefore, let us look at some characteristics of mental health, rather than illness, and see how Jesus squares with those standards.

The Picture of Health

The National Association for Mental Health has issued a brief pamphlet for laymen, entitled *Mental Health Is*.[106] In it are listed ''some of the characteristics of people with good mental health.'' These are then divided into three groups of qualities:

1. They feel comfortable about themselves.
2. They feel right about other people.
3. They are able to meet the demands of life.

These qualities are then elaborated upon in turn with descriptions such as the following:*

1. Mentally healthy people can control their emotions such as those of fear, anger, love, jealousy, guilt, or worry. They have a good sense of self-respect, recognizing the extent of their abilities and accepting their shortcomings and disappointments. They are able to deal rationally and realistically with most situations that come their way. They are able to laugh at themselves and obtain satisfaction from simple everyday pleasures.

In comparing aspects of Jesus' personality with the above attributes, we see that Jesus had a good sense of self-esteem. He clearly understood his mission. ''For the Son of Man has come to seek and to save that which was lost'' (Luke 19:10). He had a perfect concept of timing as it related to his ministry. To his mother he said, ''My hour has not yet come'' (John 2:4). He knew when to avoid danger. ''He was unwilling to walk in Judea, because the Jews were seeking to kill

---

*The descriptions have been moderately amplified by the author.

Him'' (John 7:1). To his brothers he said, ''Go up to the feast yourselves; I do not go up to this feast because My time has not yet fully come'' (John 7:8).

2. Mentally healthy people are able to give love and have consideration for the interests of others. They like and trust others and expect to be liked and trusted by others in return. They respect differences of opinion in others and do not push their own onto them. They feel a part of a group, have a sense of responsibility toward their neighbors, and are able to develop satisfying relationships and lasting friendships.

Jesus was unequivocally committed to the needs of others. In addition to his numerous healing miracles, he showed amazing skill as a counselor or therapist: with Nicodemus (John 3); with the woman at the well (John 4); with the Bethany family of Mary, Martha, and Lazarus (John 11 and 12); and with his disciples (John 12-17).

Also, he fed the hungry five thousand (recorded in all four Gospels) and restored sanity to the maniac of Gadara (Mark 5:1-20). While enduring the excruciating physical pain of hanging on the cross, he arranged for his mother to be taken care of (John 19:25-27) and was able to comfort and reassure one of the criminals being crucified alongside him (Luke 23:39-43).

3. Mentally healthy people are able to accept their responsibilities, cope with their problems, change undesirable elements of their environment whenever possible, or accept the unchangeable, if necessary, without resentment. They plan ahead, not fearing the future. They set realistic goals for themselves. They use their natural abilities to the fullest, thereby attaining satisfaction and fulfillment. They think and decide for themselves, welcoming new ideas but not rejecting old ones found from experience to be tested and true.

Jesus fully met the demands of living and fulfilled all his earthly responsibilities, including that of teaching the better way. He condemned the self-righteous, hypocritical Pharisees who led others astray (Matt. 23:1-36), yet at the same time he felt compassion for the Jerusalem that rejected him: ''How often I wanted to gather your children together, the way a hen gathers

In the same way, he felt a heaviness of heart over the rich young ruler. Jesus had sharp insight into the young man's problem, which was his love of material wealth and comfort. "And looking at him, Jesus felt a love for him, and said to him, 'One thing you lack: go and sell all you possess, and give it to the poor, and you shall have treasure in heaven; and come, follow Me.' But at these words his face fell, and he went away grieved, for he was one who owned much property" (Mark 10:21-22).

Jesus' mental health is nowhere better exemplified than in his teachings. The Sermon on the Mount is still the best summary of principles for living. Fisher and Hawley have ventured to say:

> If you were to take the sum total of all authoritative articles ever written by the most qualified of psychologists and psychiatrists on the subject of mental hygiene, if you were to take the whole of the meat and none of the parsley and if you were to have all of these unadulterated bits of pure scientific knowledge precisely expressed by the most capable poets you would have an awkward and incomplete summation of the Sermon on the Mount and it would suffer immeasurably through comparison.[107]

Psychotherapy today uses many of the principles of Jesus' teaching. In contrast to the growing spirit of self-pampering narcissism in our own time, Jesus' principle of self-love means having a good sense of self-worth, esteem, or respect for onself. This is the vital prerequisite for obeying the commandment "You shall love your neighbor as yourself" (Matt. 22:39).

In addition, the practice of forgiveness is essential to all healthy interpersonal relationships (Matt. 18:21-22), as is the so-called Golden Rule of doing to others what you would desire that they do to you (Luke 6:31).

Can we rely on the incidents and encounters through which we have evaluated the mental health of Jesus? Only the most rank skepticism would still deny the authenticity of these accounts. In *What Can We Know About Jesus?* liberal theologian Ferdinand Hahn describes how the stripping away process of even the most radical biblical critics leaves the major picture of Jesus intact. He cites Bornkamm's book on Jesus[108] as an example and then shows that in what is left ''we encounter in the minstry of Jesus . . . a claim and an authority which testify to use of the proximity and the living power of God.''[109]

A person is free to maintain that Jesus, out of honest delusion, made his claim to deity. But if one takes this position, he does so without any psychological evidence in its support and, indeed, in spite of considerable evidence to the contrary.

chapter seven

A Change of Venue for Jesus

*Concluding remarks are made about the relative prob-
abilities of a purely human and a divine Jesus. Any consideration of supernatural revelation poses certain problems
to the modern mind. These philosophical and intellectual
problems are briefly addressed.*

A *change of venue*, says the dictionary, is a change
in the location of a trial for purposes of the fairest
possible hearing. This book is a call for a change of
venue for Jesus. The authors respectfully submit that
evidences in favor of the deity of Jesus abound. Certainly the evidence is sufficient for individuals to consider it themselves, rather than deferring to the views
of popular theological movements.

What has been seen in the foregoing discussion is
not simply that "experts" can be wrong. We all knew
that. But more, we also see that a bold a priori
rationalism has served, not as a prelude to freeing men   103

of religious prejudices, but instead as a powerful source of prior commitments itself. One wonders how many years our "theological round trip" would have taken, had the theory of late-dating the New Testament faced the normal demands for evidence that other theories face. There is, of course, no way to answer that question. But it remains for us now to reopen the evaluation of Jesus under new and clarified circumstances. Our choices have been greatly simplified now that we know, beyond any reasonable doubt, that Jesus did indeed seize title to deity.

At this point, some may be saying, "Well, I see the force of your argument. It doesn't make sense to maintain that Jesus was a liar, nor does it make sense to relegate him to the ranks of the mentally ill. But isn't there some middle ground? Isn't it possible to believe in an honest, mentally healthy Jesus as a great teacher of humanity, yet one who was only a man?" It cannot be denied that this is the precise view to which multitudes of people have grown *accustomed*. For that reason, it may be the view that many will prefer. Nevertheless, it is, in the very nature of the case, the only *impossible* option. Jesus' insistent words remove the "middle" ground on which such an option would stand. Stauffer himself points out how Jesus' personal presence and the immediacy of the phenomenon with which his audience was confronted brought about this same sharp focus of alternatives:

> Jesus had said all this not as though it were apocalyptic speculation that could be greeted with belief or disbelief, but with the transcendent authority of a great stranger from another world, so that individuals believed or disbelieved in him. He spoke of belief in the Son of Man and accepted worship. To one who spoke thus it is only possible to reply yes or no.[110]

Although we have shown the extreme improbability of Jesus being either a liar or a lunatic, someone may protest, "I still say it is *possible* that Jesus was a liar" or, "It's *possible* that he was a lunatic." And this is true. Either is a possible conclusion we can make. The question of highest significance, however, is not which of the three alternatives is possible, but which is *most*

probable? We must, of course, come to our own conclusions on the matter. But in the process we must strip
away the insulation of time and pay honest intellectual
tribute to the evidence.

However, there is something besides evidence. It
may well be that another factor is at work in our
suspicion of the supernatural conclusion. Such a conclusion introduces us to a dimension with which we
may easily feel at loose ends. We are apt to struggle
with a realm that we cannot measure or weigh, that
does not submit to the bar of our reason, and that defies
our otherwise quite adequate categories. In short, it is a
dimension where we seem unable to get any "mental
traction."

The problem here is well illustrated by an intriguing
little book by Edwin Abbott entitled *Flatland: A Romance of Many Dimensions*. Abbott describes a quaint
world of but two dimensions (called Flatland), inhab-
ited by squares, triangles, circles, pentagons, etc.
Within their two dimensions, these natives of Flatland
live an otherwise quite normal existence, with homes,
jobs, and all the activities and detail of our own lives.

But, in the middle of the book, a very unnerving
experience occurs to the narrator and main character,
A. Square.[111] He is visited by a stranger from a place
called Spaceland. The stranger claims he is a Sphere (a
meaningless term to A. Square), yet as he intersects
Flatland and interacts with A. Square, he appears to A.
Square to be a circle (see Figure 5). A. Square knows
that there's something quite unusual about him (although he has the *voice* of a mere circle) because the
Sphere first appears to A. Square to be a small dot, and
then grows into a circle of a larger and larger diameter.

The conversation between A. Square and the Sphere
is classic. The Sphere does his best to describe to A.
Square where he is from, but finds himself constantly
resorting to words like "up" and "down," "above,"
and the like, words that have no meaning for A.
Square. Interspersed with long sighs, the conversation
deteriorates with the exasperation of the Sphere and the

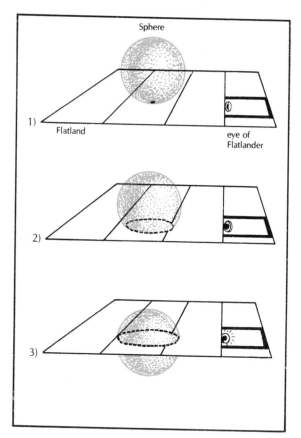

Figure 5. A Sphere
entering Flatland, as
seen by the eye of
a two-dimensional
Flatlander. As the
Sphere passes
through Flatland, the
Flatlander first views
it only as a dot, then
as an expanding cir-
cle, but not as a
Sphere.

impatience of A. Square. As a matter of fact, it seems
to be coming to a total impasse, when the Sphere
finally realizes he will have to resort to deeds if he is to
be successful in communicating to A. Square about
Spaceland. He takes A. Square right out of his plane of
existence *into Spaceland with him.* Only then does
A. Square comprehend what the Sphere was trying to
communicate. For the first time, A. Square gazes at the
Sphere and sees that he is much more than a circle. He
marvels at the beauty and symmetry of the Sphere,

finally realizing that it was the Sphere's intersection with Flatland that caused him to *appear* as a circle, even though he was much more than that all along.

The power of this enjoyable little book is simply its demonstration of A. Square's plight. He was confronted with a presence that his world—the one he felt and saw and learned of all of his life—had no dimension to accommodate. With no previous experience of the third dimension, how could A. Square help but be mystified by one who claims sphericity?

It is a short but precarious step from mystification to prejudice. It has become common practice to banish what we cannot understand. Accordingly, in the absence of any intrinsic impossibility, many have nevertheless stricken deity and the supernatural from their world view.

A Sonnet of Revelation

Unlike the Sphere's visit to Flatland, however, Jesus' visit to the human race was not totally unannounced. As a matter of fact, there have been other lights from beyond "the veil," and Jesus' appearance to mankind is the climax of an entire sonnet of revelation to man. Here, in summary, is the major progression of that sonnet:

Nature. The biblical view teaches that the natural world around us is an evidence of God's creative genius (Rom. 1:20). We are told that the heavens declare the glory of God (Ps. 19:1). Our recognition of this seems to be intuitive. Even the songwriter says, "Nothing comes from nothing; nothing ever could." And no matter how keen our scientific knowledge becomes, we are left with the same conclusion. The laws of thermodynamics back up the songwriter. All indications to date are that the universe has a finite age, but no material cause has yet been successfully proposed for its origin, its structure, or its beauty. Material reality then is an effect—an unceasing evidence of some immaterial cause. For the searching inhabitants of "Materialand," it provides provocative suggestion of an additional dimension.

Mankind. There is much about man himself that reflects his Creator. According to the book of Genesis, man and woman were created in the image of God (Gen. 1:27). We can look at man and truly marvel at him. Look at the fascinating order of his mind, his creative energy, and his moral sensitivity. To be sure, there is cruelty and evil, but these do not hide the mountain peaks. Man's sense of right and wrong may vary from one time and place to another, from people to people, and between individuals. But nowhere do we see man without the inescapable sense that some things are right and others are wrong. Even the brute materialist will say his piece against hypocrisy—for example, hypocrisy like that of a fraudulent Jesus. Yet if we do not allow ultimate reality to be moral, then we cannot morally condemn anyone or anything. If everything is the product of matter and energy operating through time by chance, who is to say "such and such is right or wrong"? Yet the materialist goes on with his value judgments. He does so because his intuitive feel for rightness and wrongness—though often marred or obscured—is a part of God's moral image within and has its source in the very One denied. And just as the Sphere was pictured in part by the circles of Flatland, so man bears in part the image of God.

The History of Israel. On this stage of natural revelation, i.e, the evidences of God in creation and in man, there has been played out the unfolding saga of the history of Israel. The history of this small nation has been uniquely stamped by the dealings of God with mankind. Time after time God spoke to Israel through her prophets. These messages—of love, of instruction, of warning, of guidance—served as the central nervous system of Israel. In order that Israel might know these messages were from God, they came in the divine vehicle of prophetic utterances. The prophets of Israel were able to foretell future events, both events of their own generation and those to be fulfilled in explicit detail hundreds of years later. So remarkable has been their predictive power, that skeptics have claimed the prophecies were "pious forgeries" and must have been written after the predicted events while posing as much earlier writings. The allegations have not stood, but the compliment has.

Messianic Prophecy. No ambassador from one nation to another would simply show up in its capital city without some advance introduction. Just so, we may expect that if God planned to enter the human race, He would earlier describe the credentials that we could look for. Thus, flowing out of these same prophetic writings have been the prophecies of a coming Messiah. Jesus said that the Hebrew Scriptures spoke of him (John 5:39); and sixty-one to seventy-one of the messianic prophecies, depending on the methods of counting, were fulfilled in the birth, life, and death of Jesus.[112] The odds that one person could fortuitously fulfill even half of these by sheer chance are so remote as to be unthinkable. Yet, when we eliminate all prophecies that he conceivably could have fulfilled by manipulating circumstances, we still must account for more than half. It is not easy to arrange for one's birth in Bethlehem (Micah 5:2; Luke 2:4-7) or to be of the lineage of the House of David (Jer. 23:5; Luke 2:23, 31). Thus the prophecies that could not be engineered mount and, taken together, offer our time-locked minds further evidences of a dimension beyond the natural.

The Miracles of Jesus. Finally we come to Jesus himself, the centerpiece of the human race. There is his charisma, his contagious personality, to be sure. But there are also his miraculous works. Here too, we have intriguing evidence. R. E. D. Clark has shown the importance of psychological studies of the congenitally blind as they bear on the Mark 8 account of Jesus' healing of the blind man.[113] Clark cites the work of M. von Senden entitled *Space and Sight*.[114] Von Senden studied some eighty cases of adults whose congenital cataracts were surgically removed. In so doing, he learned that those who grew up without sight had a conceptually different idea of space and dimensions. Specifically, they categorized things according to structural schema. One prominent schema included both men and trees, which are grouped together because the basic structure of both is that of a trunk with limbs. In Mark 8:24, the blind man whom Jesus healed remarked, "I see men, for I am seeing them like trees walking about." Von Senden cites the specific comparison of men to trees made by these patients, both before and after receiving their sight. The words of a man just given his sight could not bear a more authentic ring than those of the man Jesus healed in Mark 8:24.

But to Jesus, his miraculous works are secondary (John 6:28-35); he did not flaunt them. And as we have said earlier, not even his enemies *denied* them.[115] They simply claimed he drew supernatural power from an evil source.

A Conclusion. We should note that Jesus' miracles alone would be insufficient to lead us to a clear conclusion of his deity. Fortunately, however, his miracles were never presented alone, but in concert with his completion of the messianic prophecies, his behavior, and his own indelible claims.

Yes, the claim of Jesus may confront us with an uneasy feeling about the possibility of encountering another realm. The fear may loom that, without a reference point, it will be difficult to find mental footing on such ground. The foregoing sonnet of revelation, however, supplies many points of contact—mental and rational precedents—within our material realm for a dimension beyond our own. Within this frame of reference it seems most reasonable to judge that Jesus was not a liar or a lunatic, but that indeed a Great Visitor from beyond Materialand has broken in upon us.

If this is so, then the words of Jesus take on an altogether new significance. If he is who he claimed to be, then his teachings—the propositional content of that revelation of God to man—provide an integration point for all of reality and, most importantly, for *our* reality—the perplexities, problems, and circumstances of our lives. James Stewart relates the account of a day

when death had darkened the home of that rugged but sensitive soul, Thomas Carlyle. Someone taking a New Testament opened it at the Gospel of St. John and read the familiar words: "Let not your heart be troubled, in my

Father's house are many mansions." "Aye," muttered the bereaved man, "if you were God you had a right to say that, but if you were only a man what do you know any more than the rest of us?"[116]

If what Jesus says of himself is true, then what he says of mankind is true, as well, and thus has tremendous implications for all. What greater reason could there be for a new fascination with Jesus of Nazareth? If God has paid us a visit, this event of history deserves our most careful and sincere consideration.

The Relation
of Messiahship
to Deity

The average person today with even passing exposure to orthodox Christianity makes no great distinction between prophecies and claims of messiahship and prophecies and claims of deity. To most, the two are interchangeable or at least inseparable. This conception is derived from the fact that Christian teaching has long held Jesus to be both Messiah and deity.

However, there was no similar wedding of the two in the mind of the first-century Jew. He awaited impatiently the appearance of Messiah, but he did not identify that expectation with the personality of God Himself, as seen in passages of the Old Testament.

It is noteworthy that the term *Son of God,* held so commonly today to refer to deity,[117] meant only "Messiah" to Jewish ears of the first century. Although the New Testament writers taught the deity of Jesus, they too understood the term Son of God in the same sense that it was understood by any first-century Jew (i.e., Messiah, not deity). However, the New Testament meaning was enriched by revelations that came with certain significant events in Jesus' life. Thus the sonship *inherited* from King David (i.e., Messiahship) (Luke 1:27, 35) grew, as in the *announced* sonship of Jesus at his baptism (Luke 3:22) and at the Transfiguration (Luke 9:28, 35), gathering fullness clear through to the *declared* sonship of the resurrection (Rom. 1:4).

Before turning to the New Testament, let us look carefully at the Jewish concept of Messiah. We should understand first that Messiah was a much-discussed

The Jewish Conception of Messiah

subject. The Jewish scholar S. W. Baron notes, "In every case the messianic ideal dominated religious discussions, both in Palestine and in the Diaspora" (Jewish communities scattered beyond Palestine).[118]

This may be one reason the Hellenistic world shared in the expectation of a Judean king for the whole world. Even the Roman historians knew about this. In the days of Vespasian, Seutonius could write, "There had spread over all the Orient an old and established belief, that it was fated at that time for men coming from Judea to rule the world."[119] Tacitus tells of the same belief: "There was a firm persuasion . . . that at this very time the East was to grow powerful, and rulers coming from Judea were to acquire a universal empire."[120] The Jews had the belief that "about that time one from their country should become governor of the habitable earth."[121] Even Virgil, the Roman poet, writing his fourth ecologue, which is known as the *Messianic Ecologue,* spoke of the golden days to come.

The picture portrayed in *Psalms of Solomon* (45 B.C.), however, is that of a hero who would reunite Israel, restore the lost tribes, and purge Jerusalem from the trampling of the Gentiles.[122]

In the *Ethiopic Enoch* Messiah is seen as a righteous warrier, "the Son of Man who hath righteousness . . . shall loosen the reins [loins] of the strong and break the teeth of the sinners."[123] This is not unlike the picture of Daniel 7, or the picture of the Zealots, who expected military leadership from Messiah, who would appear with sword in hand. Others, visionaries of coming events, however, expected to see a new humanity marching as the aftermath of a cosmic cataclysm.[124]

Other facets of Messiah were seen in his expected reign. The Syriac *Apocalypse of Baruch* (A.D. 70-80), for example, saw an extravagant fruitfulness under the reign of Messiah.[125] He, it was believed, would protect his people from the reign of sin[126] and would rule over disputes with an intuitive sense of justice.[127]

Yet for all of this, at the time of Jesus, there was no hint of belief in a divine Messiah. As J. Klausner said in *The Messianic Idea in Israel,* "The Jewish Messiah is truly human in origin, of flesh and blood like all mortals."[128] The closest that one comes to the idea of a divine Messiah (in the Jewish expectations of the day) is in the Talmudic *Baraitha* and in "Parables" of the *Ethiopic Enoch,* both of which indicate that the name of Messiah was created before the world. This has little to do, however, with a divine Messiah. At most, Messiah was to them a purely human instrument in the hands of God.[129]

The New Testament Conception of Messiah

Jewish scholars have taught that the New Testament concept of Messiah took wings from the Jewish idea then current of a political deliverer or redeemer.[130] The New Testament, they say, expands the idea of physical redemption for Israel—in need of relief from her foreign oppressors—to the idea of spiritual redemption for all the world. The role of Messiah is, of course, central to the idea of redemption. The intensely felt longing for a political deliverer is certainly evident in the pages of the Gospels, and we can see there its influence on the Jews' response to Jesus.

The crucial question, however, is, *Do we see the idea of spiritual redemption for all the world in the messianic passages of the Old Testament?* The question has long been debated. The late Alfred Edersheim, who was the Grinfield Lecturer on the Septuagint at Oxford University, gave effective evidence that the idea is as native to the Old Testament as it is to the New.[131]

Nevertheless, the Jews of the first century were not looking for a spiritual deliverer for their pagan neighbors, but a political liberator for themselves. The figure cut by Jesus was not what they were looking for. Yale University's Millar Burrows said, "Jesus was so unlike what all Jews expected the son of David to be that his own disciples found it almost impossible to connect the idea of the Messiah with him."[132]

Amplifying this theme in *Sketches of Jewish Social Life in the Days of Christ,* Edersheim showed the impossibility of tracing Christianity to the Sadducees, Pharisees, or Essenes.[133] He further commented on how unexpected was a Messiah who neither wished to increase the wall of partition between Jew and Gentile nor even to pull the Gentile over the wall, but who wanted rather to destroy the wall altogether, removing the alienation of the Jewish Law. Edersheim rightly said, "There was nothing analogous to it; not a hint of it to be found, either in the teaching or the spirit of the times. Quite the opposite. Assuredly, the most unlike thing to Christ were His times."[134]

**The Deity of
Messiah in the
Old Testament**

A second point of major interest is whether or not the Old Testament legitimately can be said to teach the deity of Messiah. We will look briefly at five passages that are relevant, providing also one or more Jewish interpretations of each passage from Klausner, Baron, or Amram. The reader is reminded that these are only a few of the wealth of messianic passages, in particular, those from which the Jew could have seen a glimpse of Messiah's deity.

First, Isaiah 9:6, "For a child will be born to us, a son will be given to us; and the government will rest on His shoulders; And His name will be called Wonderful Counselor, Mighty God, Eternal Father, Prince of Peace."

There is no doubt that this is a classic messianic passage. On first reading, it would seem to be an indisputable reference to the deity of the "child," the "son." Yet, in view of the use of the Hebrew terms elsewhere, it is possible to render "Mighty God" (Hebrew, *el gibber*) as "Mighty Warrior." Although this is in keeping with Jewish messianic expectation, it stands in curious contrast to "Prince of Peace."

It is interesting that some have seen two Messiahs in Isaiah 9:6—Messiah ben Joseph and the Messiah ben David, the King of Peace. It was said, "When the King Messiah is revealed to Israel, he will not open his mouth except for peace, as it is written (Isa. 52:7), 'How lovely on the mountains are the feet of him who brings good news, who announces peace.' "[135] So in this case, Messiah was divided into two, because of the perplexity of the apparent contradiction in a Messiah who would be a "Mighty Warrior" and a "Prince of

Peace." Could it not be that a "Mighty God" would wear the title "Prince of Peace" with more ease?

It is also possible to render "Eternal Father" (Hebrew, *abi-ad*) as a title of benevolence conferred upon a favored king, rather than taking its meaning at face value. There is certainly nothing wrong with entertaining legitimate alternative readings such as these, although many scholars take the position that the apparent meanings are in fact the intent of the writer. In his refutation of Schonfield, for example, Edwin Yamauchi argues for the latter position.[136]

Klausner's interpretation is simply that the child or son is not the "Mighty God" or the "Eternal Father," but little reason is given for this apparent turning of the passage.[137]

Next, we turn to a passage that, we grant, can only be suggestive of Messiah's deity. Yet it is an important passage, one that shows the dilemma of a Messiah whose "prophetic credentials" were only half read. Isaiah 53 has long been held by Christian scholars to be messianic—a picture of the Suffering Servant. The psalm presents the suffering of one "as a guilt offering" (verse 10) to "bear their iniquities" (verse 11). Yet within this theme (one not likely to be recognized as messianic through the "political filter" of beleaguered Israel) is the subtheme of conquering: "And He will divide the booty with the strong" (verse 12). Edersheim points out that suffering is human, while conquering is divine; yet to *conquer by suffering,* as in Isaiah 53, is theanthropic (God-manlike).

Concerning Isaiah 53, Edersheim relates the perplexity of Jewish interpreters. From Pusey's "Preface to the Catena of Jewish Interpretations on the 53rd of Isaiah," he quotes Ibn Amram, "There is no little difficulty in giving a sense to those most obscure words of Isaiah, they manifestly need a prophetic spirit."[138]

The traditional Jewish interpretation that the Suffering Servant is Israel, rather than a personal Messiah, runs afoul when, as a substitute (verse 8), the Servant takes the stroke due to "my people" (Israel). Under this interpretation, we would have Israel substituting for Israel!

Psalm 45 is another intriguing passage. Here the psalmist is extolling the virtues and deeds of "the King." Suddenly he sets his addressee apart from any human ruler. "Thy throne O God, is forever and ever" (verse 6). He goes on to say, "Thou hast loved righteousness, and hated wickedness; Therefore God, Thy God, has anointed Thee with the oil of joy above Thy fellows" (verse 7). Here is a ruler who has "fellows" among men, is addressed as no less than God, a God with an eternal reign.

Next, consider Psalm 110:1, as developed in the text of chapter two. Jesus employs this passage (see Mark 12:35-37) to stretch the messianic concept of the scribes and Pharisees. He confronts them with the problem of David (the psalmist) writing of "the son of David" (Messiah), calling him "my Lord."

Although Psalm 110:1 had to be underscored by Jesus, there is in the Midrash a combination of this passage with Daniel 7:13, just as Jesus used them in Mark 14:62 before the Sanhedrin. Lane's footnote is given:

> The midrashic combination of Dan. 7:13 with Ps. 110:1 occurs in the Midrash on Psalms on Ps. 2:7 (i. 40, § 9) and on Ps. 18 (i. 261, § 29). In the first passage Ps. 2:7 is linked with texts from the Torah, the Writings and the Prophets: "And in one place in the Writings it says, 'The Eternal One said to my Lord, "Sit at my right hand"'' (Ps. 110:1), and it says: 'The Eternal One said to me, "You are my Son"' (Ps. 2:7). And in another place it says, 'See, one came with the clouds of heaven, as a Son of Man' (Dan 7:13)."[139]

Finally, we turn to Daniel 7:13-28. This passage has been given a variety of interpretations. Apparently written during the exile in Babylon, the predictive power of this passage over the ensuing centuries has been so great that some have taken it as "pious forgery" merely posing as an early work pretending to predict what it in fact must have reported.[140] Yamauchi[141] and others, however, have shown that Daniel cannot date later than the time claimed for it.[142] Baron sees in the passage the successive kingdoms of

Babylon, Persia, Greece, and Rome, and then the coming of Messiah; whereas Klausner sees no personal Messiah in the passage, but rather the nation Israel.

Neither Baron nor Klausner discusses the identification of the Son of Man with the Ancient of Days near the chapter's end. In this chapter, we see "one like the Son of Man" being presented to "the Ancient of Days" (God). The Son of Man is given an everlasting dominion. Later in the passage, this everlasting dominion is said to belong to the "Highest One" (verse 27), which is a definitive reference to deity.

It can be seen from the foregoing brief survey that the idea of a Messiah who is also deity is no stranger to the Old Testament. A divine Messiah is as much at home in the Old Testament as he is in the New.

Response

The New Testament theologians were, by upbring- **F. F. BRUCE**
ing, orthodox Jews. For men such as these, the language used about Jesus in the New Testament was not the kind of language that it was permissible to use of any man. That they used it nevertheless, and used it spontaneously, as though it were the most fitting language in the world to apply to Jesus, bears witness to the impact that he made on his immediate followers, and through them on others.

For Paul, Jesus is the image of God, the one in whom "all the fulness of Deity dwells in bodily form" (Col. 2:9). Yet Paul clearly distinguishes between Jesus and God the Father: "For us there is but one God, the Father, . . . and one Lord, Jesus Christ" (1 Cor. 8:6). But when Jesus is called "one Lord," it is made plain that this is the name above every name, conferred on him by God, which entitles him to share the worship that is properly paid to God alone.

The writer to the Hebrews recognizes Jesus as the one to whom the words of Psalm 45:6 are addressed: "Thy throne, O God, is forever and ever." But here too the distinction between him and God the Father is carefully maintained: "Therefore, God, Thy God, hath anointed Thee . . ." (Heb. 1:9). The Father is the anointer; the Son is the anointed one.

For John the evangelist, Jesus is the eternal Word or self-expression of God, become flesh for the world's salvation. As such, he was in the beginning with God, but at the same time he was God, or (as the New English Bible puts it) "what God was, the Word was" (John 1:1).

Our two authors recognize that the mind of Jesus 121

himself, and not simply the reflections of the New
Testament theologians, must be studied if the question
of Jesus' true identity is to receive a satisfactory answer. They recognize, too, that if the mind of Jesus is
to be historically ascertained, a critical study of the
Gospels is necessary. Some who hold to the historical
accuracy of the Gospels have feared that a critical
study of them can only result in blemishing their validity. Let it be clearly understood that if the Gospels are
historically reliable, their critical study can only
confirm their reliability.

This study uses three forms of criticism. Literary
criticism explores the literary interrelation of the Gospels and tries to discover such documentary sources as
may lie behind them. Form criticism aims at getting
behind the written documents and reaching conclusions about the transmission of their material in the oral
stage. It is interested also in the life setting of this
material—its original life setting in the ministry of
Jesus and the subsequent life setting in which it was
selected, shaped, and arranged in primitive Christian
worship and witness. Redaction criticism studies the
way in which the respective evangelists used and presented the gospel material that they received.

So far as the subject of this work is concerned, the
upshot of such criticial study regarding the person of
Jesus was summed up forty years ago by C. H. Dodd in
these words:

> It is not doubtful that from the beginning the tradition
> affirmed that He lived, taught, worked, suffered and died
> as Messiah. We can find no alternative tradition, excavate
> as we will in the successive strata of the Gospels.[143]

But if the tradition affirmed this, what did Jesus
himself affirm? It seems evident that, throughout his
public ministry, Jesus did not habitually make explicit
messianic claims for himself. Had he done so, he could
certainly have been misunderstood, as his concept of
the Messiah was poles apart from popular expectation.
Even in the Gospel of John, where Jesus is more
outspoken about his person and mission than in the
other three, the Jerusalem authorities have to ask him,

less than four months before the crucifixion, "How long will you keep us in suspense? If you are the Messiah, tell us plainly" (John 10:24).

Yet, in the synoptic Gospels also, the implications of Jesus' public utterances were not lost on discerning minds. This is particularly true of his utterances regarding the Son of Man. He may well have chosen this expression because it was not current in Judaism and therefore had no popular associations that his hearers would have to unlearn; he could fill it with whatever meaning he pleased. But the meaning with which he did fill it connoted a claim to exceptional authority.

"The Son of Man" on his lips signified "the 'One like a Son of Man' " in Daniel 7:13 to whom universal dominion is given. This is true of the first and last occurrences of the title as they are recorded in Mark's Gospel. The Son of Man has authority to forgive sins (Mark 2:10) because he has authority to execute judgment (cf. John 5:27). On the last great day the Son of Man would appear as the assessor of God. That this was appreciated by some of those who heard his reply to the high priest's question (Mark 14:62) is clear enough; it was for this, and not for any messianic claim, that he was pronounced guilty of blasphemy.

If we compare the varying synoptic versions of his reply, it seems to have amounted to this: "If *Messiah* is the word that you insist on using, then my only answer must be 'Yes, I am he'; but if I choose my own words, what I say is this: 'You shall see the Son of Man seated at the right hand of the Almighty, and coming with the clouds of heaven.' "

His judges recognized that this was, in effect, a claim to be the peer of the Most High. They did not stay to consider whether or not it was a well-founded claim; that it could be true of any man was, in their eyes, out of the question. The validity and personal implications of his claim still challenge us to a decision.

References

[1]G. R. Driver, *The Judaean Scrolls: The Problem and a Solution* (Oxford: Blackwell, 1965), p. 3.

[2]David Bohm, "Further Remarks on Order," in *Towards A Theoretical Biology,* ed. C. H. Waddington (Chicago: Aldine, 1968), p. 41.

[3]Oscar Cullmann, *Christology of the New Testament,* trans. Shirley C. Guthrie and Charles A. M. Hall (Philadelphia: Westminster, 1959), p. 307.

[4]*The Koran* 41. 6.

[5]H. D. Lewis and Robert Lawson Slater, *World Religions: Meeting Points and Major Issues* (London: C. A. Watts, 1966), p. 174.

[6]E. O. James, *Christianity and Other Religions* (Philadelphia: Lippincott, 1968), p. 170.

[7]C. S. Lewis, "What Are We to Make of Jesus Christ?" in *God in the Dock: Essays on Theology and Ethics,* ed. Walter Hooper (Grand Rapids: Eerdmans, 1970), p. 157.

[8]William L. Lane, *Commentary on the Gospel of Mark* (Grand Rapids: Eerdmans, 1974), p. 95.

[9]Ezekiel 28:2-10; Psalms of Solomon 2:28f.; Mekilta Exodus 15:7-11; Siphre Deuteronomium 21:22; and Mishnah: Sanhedrin 4:5.

[10]Ethelbert Stauffer, *Jesus and His Story,* trans. Richard and Clara Winston (New York: Knopf, 1974), p. 174; Alfred Edersheim, *The Life and Times of Jesus the Messiah,* 2 vols. (reprint ed., Grand Rapids: Eerdmans, 1962), 2:156, 159.

[11]Stauffer, *His Story,* p. 181.

[12]Ibid.

[13]Ibid.

[14]Ibid., p. 187.

[15]H. H. Cohn, *The Trial and Death of Jesus* (New York: Harper & Row, 1971).

[16]Josephus *The Wars of the Jews* 2. 8. 1.

[17]Stauffer, *His Story*, p. 208.

[18]Lane, *Mark*, p. 537.

[19]Mishnah: Sanhedrin 7:5.

[20]H. J. Schoeps, *Paul*, trans. Harold Knight (Philadelphia: Westminster, 1961), p. 162.

[21]Ezekiel 28:2ff.; Psalms of Solomon 2:28-29; Mekilta Exodus 15:7-11; Siphre Deuteronomium 21:22; and Mishnah: Sanhedrin 4:5.

[22]Stauffer, *His Story*, pp. 192-94.

[23]Eusebius *Ecclesiastical History* 3. 39.

[24]John W. Montgomery, *Where Is History Going?* (Grand Rapids: Zondervan, 1969), p. 59.

[25]Oxford Society of Historical Theology, *The New Testament in the Apostolic Fathers* (Oxford: Clarendon, 1905).

[26]Frederic Kenyon, *The Bible and Archeology* (New York: Harper, 1940), pp. 288ff.

[27]B. F. Westcott and F. J. A. Hort, *The New Testament in the Original Greek*, vol. 1 (New York: Macmillan, 1881), p. 2.

[28]John A. T. Robinson, *Redating the New Testament* (Philadelphia: Westminster, 1976), p. 3.

[29]Martin Dibelius, *Die Formgeschichte des Evangeliums* (Tübingen: Mohr, 1921).

[30]Martin Dibelius, *From Tradition to Gospel*, trans. Bertram Lee Woolf (London: Ivor Nicholson and Watson, 1934).

[31]Rudolf Bultmann, *Die Geschichte der synoptischen Tradition* (Gottingen: Vandenhoeck & Ruprecht, 1921).

[32]Rudolf Bultmann, *The History of the Synoptic Tradition*, trans. John Marsh (New York: Harper & Row, 1963).

[33]Rudolf Bultmann, "The New Approach to the Synoptic Problem," *Journal of Religion* 6 (July 1929): 341.

[34]Robinson, *Redating*, p. 359.

[35]B. P. Grenfell and A. S. Hunt, *The Oxyrhynchus Papyri*, parts 2 and 4 (London: Oxford University Press, 1899 and 1904).

[36] Clifford A. Wilson, *Rocks, Relics and Biblical Reliability* (Grand Rapids: Zondervan, 1977), pp. 115-16.

[37] William Mitchell Ramsay, *St. Paul the Traveller and Roman Citizen,* 14th ed. (London: Hodder and Stoughton, 1920), p. 4.

[38] Edwin M. Yamauchi, "First Reactions from the Scholars," an addition to *Could One Small Fragment Shake the World?* a reprint from *Eternity* (Philadelphia: Evangelical Foundation, 1972), p. 15.

[39] F. F. Bruce, "On Dating the New Testament," *Eternity* 22 (June 1972): 33.

[40] Donald Guthrie, *New Testament Introduction,* 3rd ed. (Downers Grove, Ill.: Tyndale, 1970), p. 73.

[41] Robinson, *Redating,* p. 13.

[42] Ibid., p. 275.

[43] Howard Marshall, "Palestinian and Hellenistic Christianity: Some Critical Comments," *New Testament Studies* 19 (April 1973): 271-87.

[44] William F. Albright, "Toward a More Conservative View," an interview by the editors of *Christianity Today,* 18 January 1963, p. 3.

[45] William F. Albright, *New Horizons in Biblical Research* (London: Oxford University Press, 1966), p. 46.

[46] Werner Georg Kümmel, *Introduction to the New Testament,* 17th ed., trans. Howard Clark Kee (Nashville: Abingdon, 1973), pp. 203-4.

[47] Charles Kingsley Barrett, *The Gospel According to St. John* (New York: Macmillan, 1955), pp. 14-18, 34-37.

[48] P. Gardner-Smith, *Saint John and the Synoptic Gospels* (Cambridge: Cambridge University Press, 1938).

[49] C. H. Dodd, *Historical Tradition in the Fourth Gospel* (Cambridge: Cambridge University Press, 1963).

[50] Norman L. Geisler, *Christian Apologetics* (Grand Rapids: Baker, 1976), p. 311.

[51] Joachim Jeremias, *The Rediscovery of Bethesda,* New Testament Archaeology Monograph, no. 1 (Louisville: Southern Baptist Theological Seminary, 1966), p. 38.

[52] Robinson, *Redating,* p. 275.

[53] George E. Ladd, *A Theology of the New Testament* (Grand Rapids: Eerdmans, 1974), pp. 219-20.

[54] Ethelbert Stauffer, "Historische Elemente im vierten

Evangelium" in *Bekenntnis zur Kirche: Festgabe für Ernst Sommerlath zum 70,* ed. E. H. Amberg and U. Kühn (Berlin: Sommerlath, 1960), pp. 33-51.

[55]Robinson, *Redating,* pp. 267-68.

[56]Jack Finegan, *Light from the Ancient Past* (Princeton: Princeton University Press, 1959), p. 282.

[57]Robinson, *Redating,* pp. 50-58, 84; Kümmel, *Introduction,* pp. 257, 264, 279, 293, 304, 311, 332, 348, 349; Guthrie, *Introduction,* pp. 397, 442, 464, 515, 535, 536, 558, 566, 567, 623, 639.

[58]F. F. Bruce, *The New Testament Documents: Are They Reliable?,* 5th rev. ed. (1960; reprint ed., Downers Grove, Ill.: InterVarsity, 1978), p. 79.

[59]William F. Albright, *Recent Discoveries in Bible Lands* (New York: Funk & Wagnalls, 1955), p. 136.

[60]Albright, "More Conservative View," p. 3.

[61]Ladd, *Theology,* p. 219.

[62]Guthrie, *Introduction,* p. 74.

[63]Paul Tillich, *Systematic Theology,* 3 vols. (Chicago: University of Chicago Press, 1957), 2:103.

[64]Robinson, *Redating,* p. 3.

[65]Ibid., p. 360.

[66]A. M. Sherwin-White, *Roman Society and Roman Law in the New Testament* (Oxford: Clarendon, 1963), pp. 186-93.

[67]Will Durant, *The Story of Civilization,* 10 vols. *Caesar and Christ,* 3 (New York: Simon and Schuster, 1944), p. 557.

[68]Irwin H. Linton, *A Lawyer Examines the Bible* (Boston: Wilde, 1943), pp. 43-44.

[69]Bruce, *Documents,* p. 79.

[70]Stauffer, *His Story,* pp. 168-69.

[71]James M. Robinson, *A New Quest of the Historical Jesus* (Naperville, Ill.: Allenson, 1959), p. 69.

[72]Louis Cassels, *This Fellow Jesus* (Anderson, Ind.: Warner, 1973).

[73]Bruce, *Documents,* pp. 45-46.

[74]Durant, *Caesar and Christ,* p. 556.

[75]Harold W. Hoehner, *Chronological Aspects of the Life of Christ* (Grand Rapids: Zondervan, 1977), pp. 95-114.

[76] Albert G. Harkness, "Age at Marriage and at Death in the Roman Empire," *Transactions of the American Philological Association* 27 (1896): 35-72.

[77] A. R. Burn, "Hic Breve Vivitur: A Study of the Expectation of Life in the Roman Empire," *Past and Present*, no. 4 (November 1953), pp. 2-31.

[78] Stauffer, *His Story*, p. 10.

[79] Ibid., p. 126; Edersheim, *Jesus the Messiah*, 2:589.

[80] Sanhedrin 2. 3.; Sanhedrin 89 a Baraitha; Tosephta Sanhedrin 2. 7.; Midrash Tanna debe Eliyyahu on Deuteronomy 17:13.

[81] Eusebius *Ecclesiastical History* 2. 2. 1.

[82] Justin *Dialog with Trypho* 108.

[83] Stauffer, *His Story*, p. 191.

[84] Lucian, *The Passing of Peregrinus*, trans. A.M. Harmon (Cambridge, Mass.: Harvard University Press, 1955), p. 51.

[85] Pliny the Younger *Epistles* 10. 96.

[86] Stauffer, *His Story*, p. 191.

[87] Yalkut Shimoni, § 776 on Numbers 23.

[88] Jerusalem Talmud: Ta'anith 2:1.

[89] Stauffer, *His Story*, p. x.

[90] Ibid., p. 185.

[91] *Ascension of Isaiah*, translated by R. H. Charles.

[92] Durant, *Caesar and Christ*, p. 557.

[93] Joseph Klausner, *From Jesus to Paul*, trans. William F. Stinespring (New York: Macmillan, 1943), p. 260.

[94] *The Koran*, Al-Imran, v.45.

[95] Fredrick C. Grant, "Jesus Christ," *An Encyclopedia of Religion*, ed. Vergilius Ferm (New York: The Philosophical Library, 1945), p. 392.

[96] C. S. Lewis, *Mere Christianity* (New York: Macmillan, 1952), pp. 55-56.

[97] Durant, *Caesar and Christ*, p. 557.

[98] Lewis, "Christ," *Dock*, pp. 157-58.

[99] W. E. H. Lecky, *History of European Morals from Augustus to Charlemagne*, 2nd ed., 2 vols. (London: Longmans, Green, 1869), 2:88.

[100] R. R. Palmer, *History of the Modern World* (New York:

Knopf, 1953), p. 11.

[101] As cited in *The Readers Digest Great Encyclopedic Dictionary* (Pleasantville, N.Y.: Readers Digest, 1975), p. 2038.

[102] Maurice Wiles, "Christianity Without Incarnation?" in *The Myth of God Incarnate,* ed. John Hick (London: SCM, 1977), p. 4.

[103] American Psychiatric Association, *A Psychiatric Glossary* (New York: Basic Books, 1975), p. 127.

[104] Ibid., p. 113.

[105] Ibid., pp. 4-5, 9.

[106] *Mental Health Is,* The National Association for Mental Health, New York, 1964.

[107] J. T. Fisher and L. S. Hawley, *A Few Buttons Missing* (Philadelphia: Lippincott, 1951), p. 273.

[108] Günther Bornkamm, *Jesus of Nazareth,* trans. Irene and Frazer McLuskey with James Robinson (New York: Harper & Row, 1959).

[109] Ferdinand Hahn, *What Can We Know About Jesus?* trans. Grover Folex (Philadelphia: Fortress, 1969), pp. 45-46.

[110] Stauffer, *His Story,* p. 165.

[111] Edwin A. Abbott, *Flatland: A Romance of Many Dimensions* (New York: Barnes and Noble, 1963), pp. 68ff.

[112] Josh McDowell, *Evidence That Demands a Verdict* (San Bernardino: Campus Crusade for Christ, 1972), pp. 151-74; J. Barton Payne, *Encyclopedia of Biblical Prophecy* (New York: Harper, 1973), pp. 665-68.

[113] R. E. D. Clark, "Men As Trees Walking," *Faith and Thought* 95 (1963): 88-94.

[114] M. von Senden, *Space and Sight: The Perception of Space and Shape in the Congenitally Blind before and after Operation,* trans. Peter Heath (New York: Methuen, 1960), 42S, cited in Clark, "Trees Walking."

[115] Stauffer, *His Story,* pp. 4-5, 9-10.

[116] James S. Stewart, *The Strong Name* (Edinburgh: T. and T. Clark, 1941), p. 80.

[117] Lane, *Mark,* p. 535.

[118] S. W. Baron, *A Social and Religious History of the Jews,* 2d ed., 2 vols. (New York: Columbia University Press, 1952), 2:58.

[119]Seutonius *Life of Vespasian* 4. 5.

[120]Tacitus *Histories* 5. 13.

[121]Josephus *Wars* 6. 5. 4.

[122]Baron, *History,* p. 61.

[123]*Ethiopic Enoch* 46. 3-4.

[124]Baron, *History,* p. 59.

[125]Ibid., p. 60.

[126]Lane, *Mark,* p. 95.

[127]J. Klausner, *The Messianic Idea in Israel* (New York: Macmillan, 1955), p. 520.

[128]Ibid.

[129]Ibid., p. 523.

[130]Ibid., p. 519; Baron, *History,* p. 523.

[131]Alfred Edersheim, *Prophecy and History in Relation to Messiah* (New York: Randolph, 1885), pp. 160-90.

[132]Millar Burrows, *More Light on the Dead Sea Scrolls* (New York: Viking, 1958), p. 68.

[133]Alfred Edersheim, *Sketches of Jewish Social Life in the Days of Christ* (Boston: Bradley, 1876; reprint ed., Grand Rapids: Eerdmans, 1950), p. 248.

[134]Ibid., p. 29.

[135]Babylonian Talmud: Sanhedrin 97a, Derekh Erets Zuta, Chapter 11.

[136]Edwin M. Yamauchi, "Passover Plot or Easter Triumph? A Critical Review of H. Schonfield's Recent Theory," in *Christianity for the Tough Minded,* ed. John W. Montgomery (Minneapolis: Bethany Fellowship, 1973), pp. 261-71.

[137]Klausner, *Messianic Idea,* p. 64.

[138]Edersheim, *Prophecy and History,* p. 105.

[139]Lane, *Mark,* p. 537.

[140]Klausner, *Messianic Idea,* pp. 222-27.

[141]Edwin M. Yamauchi, *Greece and Babylon* (Grand Rapids: Baker, 1967).

[142]Bruce K. Waltke, "The Date of the Book of Daniel," *Bibliotheca Sacra* 133 (October-December 1976): 319-29.

[143]C. H. Dodd, *History and the Gospel* (New York: Scribner, 1938), p. 103.

For Further Reading

Bruce, F. F. **The New Testament Documents: Are They Reliable?** 5th rev. ed. Downers Grove, Ill.: InterVarsity Press, 1960.

In this concise treatment, Bruce, who is highly regarded as a professor of biblical criticism, summarizes with insight and accuracy the data and arguments surrounding the reliability of the New Testament. This book has deservedly become a classic.

Green, Michael, ed. **The Truth of God Incarnate.** Sevenoaks, Kent, U.K.: Hodder, 1977; Grand Rapids: Eerdmans, 1977.

This book by five theologians is an able answer to the work **The Myth of God Incarnate.** *It contains useful sections on Jesus and myth, history, historical skepticism, and the New Testament. It is a must for those interested in the current controversy about the deity of Christ.*

Hoehner, Harold W. **Chronological Aspects of the Life of Christ.** Grand Rapids: Zondervan, 1977.

Several problems have existed over the years in pinpointing various major events in the life of Christ. In this book, a rising authority on the times of Christ summarizes the various views and brings biblical, historical, and astronomical data to resolve these dilemmas in a careful yet readable treatment.

Marshall, I. Howard. **I Believe in the Historical Jesus.** Grand Rapids: Eerdmans, 1977; London: Hodder, 1977.

Marshall discusses the problems involved in attempting to apply historical study methods to objects of worship and religious veneration. He then focuses on the study of the 133 *historical Jesus and whether or not such study can be accomplished successfully. Two views of the evidence about Jesus are taken to task: that which dismisses the evidence as fiction and that which accepts every detail without question. Although he does not accept the total accuracy of Scripture, Marshall does believe that Jesus lived, had a ministry, died, and was resurrected, and that the evidence for these facts is substantially reproduced in the Gospels.*

Marshall, I. Howard. **Origins of New Testament Christology.** Downers Grove, Ill.: InterVarsity Press, 1976; Leicester: Inter-Varsity Fellowship, 1977.

This is the first volume in the "Issues in Contemporary Theology" series. Marshall surveys the last twenty years of scholarship and interpretation regarding New Testament Christology (the study of Christ).

Martin, W. J. **The Deity of Christ.** Rev. ed. Chicago: Moody Press, 1974.

This short treatment of the topic will be helpful to the reader in search of a brief survey of the numbers of evidences of Jesus' deity. It specifically considers the ancient Aryan controversy (4th century, A.D.) on the topic, as well as modern-day parallels.

McDowell, Josh. **Evidence That Demands a Verdict.** San Bernardino, Calif.: Campus Crusade for Christ, 1972.

This book is primarily a catalog of various evidences concerning the historical validity of the Christian faith. Although it is not designed for casual reading, its outline format places an abundance of data at one's fingertips.

Moule, C. F. C. **The Origin of Christology.** New York: Cambridge University Press, 1977.

Moule writes to disprove the assumption that Christology, as developed in the New Testament and in the course of Christian history, has evolved away from the historical Jesus. Instead of such evolution, Moule argues that Christology is the drawing out and articulation of what was already there in Jesus—"the development of true insights into the original."

Stauffer, Ethelbert, **Jesus and His Story.** New York: Alfred A. Knopf, 1974.

In this important volume, Stauffer shows how Jesus' deliber-ate and unequivocal claim to deity brought him into escalat-ing conflict with Jewish authorities, climaxing in his crucifix-ion. Stauffer's contribution is of enormous importance. Al-though the reader should understand that Stauffer does not take the position of the inerrancy of Scripture, yet he does see in Scripture reliable history. His notes and appendixes are full of helpful historical detail and insight.

Wilson, Clifford A. **Rocks, Relics and Biblical Reliability.** Grand Rapids: Zondervan, 1977.

This book discusses era by era the historical accuracy of both the Old and the New Testament, as seen through the eyes of an archaeologist. It covers over two thousand years of his-tory in an enjoyable and educational way.

Notes